BAKING
with YEAST
with Schmecks Appeal

BAKING
with YEAST
with Schmecks Appeal

EDNA STAEBLER

McGraw-Hill Ryerson
Toronto   Montreal

McClelland & Stewart
Toronto

Baking With Yeast with Schmecks Appeal

First Published in 1990 by

MCGRAW-HILL RYERSON LIMITED
330 Progress Avenue
Toronto, Canada
M1P 2Z5

MCCLELLAND & STEWART LIMITED
481 University Avenue
Suite 900
Toronto, Canada
M5G 2E9

1 2 3 4 5 6 7 8 9 0 W 9 8 7 6 5 4 3 2 1 0
ISBN 0-7710-8278-9

Canadian Cataloguing in Publication Data

Staebler, Edna, date-
    Baking with yeast with schmecks appeal

(Schmecks appeal cookbook series)
ISBN 0-7710-8278-9

1. Baking.   2. Bread.   3. Cookery, Mennonite.
4. Cookery — Ontario — Waterloo (Regional municipality).
I. Title.   II. Series: Staebler, Edna, date-
Schmecks appeal cookbook series.

TX769.S84 1990   641.8'15   C90-095478-7

Printed and bound in Canada

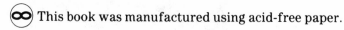 This book was manufactured using acid-free paper.

CONTENTS

INTRODUCTION

Baking with yeast is an adventure. It's more fun and more exciting than any kind of cooking I know. Something magical happens when yeast, flour, and liquid come together and are baked in a hot oven. There is nothing so intoxicating as the aroma and anticipation of crusty golden loaves, light snowy rolls, buttercakes, spicy hot cross buns, Christmas stollen, English muffins, jam-filled kuchen, sourdough biscuits and pancakes, sugar-topped coffee cakes, meat-filled piroschky, sticky Chelsea buns, Arabic pita bread, doughnuts dunked in maple syrup, pretzels, pizza, and baba au rhum.

Except during one sweltering-hot summer, I haven't bought a loaf of bread for thirty years. I've been making my own ever since a librarian came to a pot-luck supper at my cottage, brought a loaf of home-baked bread, and gave me the recipe for it. My first loaves were heavy and soggy — I admit now — but then I thought they were marvellous and kept inflicting them on all my relations till I learned better as I watched Bevvy Martin make feather-light bread that she said would stick to the ribs of her family while they worked in the barn and the fields. "If they eat store bread," she said, "they're hungry again before they've milked more than one cow."

It wonders Bevvy — and me — what the commercial bakers put — or don't put — into their bread to produce such anaemic, sponge-like slices, while a delicious, gutsy loaf of bread can be made so easily with nothing more than flour, yeast, water, and a modicum of salt, sugar, and shortening.

MAKING BREAD IS SO EASY

Though the whole process takes several hours because of the rising and baking, the actual business of mixing and kneading can be done in about twenty minutes. "But you must have the knack," people say. I think you need only an eager, experimental approach and the willingness to endure a few failures. What can you lose? A spoonful of yeast and two pounds of flour; with Canada producing millions of bushels of wheat a year, that seems no great loss. Besides, you need not have a failure. People who bake bread develop a carefree, happy confidence.

My sister, my neighbour, and a number of other people had complained to me that they'd tried and tried to make bread without success; then at last they used my seemingly fail-proof Neil's Harbour recipe, and glory be, they had beautiful, tender, high, tasty, golden loaves that stayed moist and delectable right to the end — which came all too soon.

I'm not boasting — I didn't invent it; I got the recipe from Clara May Ingraham, who made it every week for her fisherman husband and thirteen children in Neil's Harbour, Cape Breton.

Bread-making is a grand thing to do. Kneading is a kind of revelling; it makes one feel like a primitive, pioneer woman — or man — unstarvable, self-sustaining, and joyful. Bevvy sings happy hymns as she works with her yeast dough in the smooth old pine bread-trough her pioneering great-grandmother brought in a Conestoga wagon to Waterloo County. My friend Clara May, in Neil's Harbour, couldn't read or write but for sixty years she made great batches of moist, golden "buns o' bread" and always her face had a special glow on her bread-making days. My own few shrinking loaves are nothing to boast of, but I like them, and I am brazenly proud of the tender, crusty little rolls my guests apologize for eating by the dozen.

Do I seem to be trying to talk you into making your own bread? I hope you don't mind. I simply enjoy making and eating it so much myself that I'd like everyone to have the same pleasure. If, then, you can hardly wait to get started, I assure you again you are ready for one of the great satisfactions of a lifetime. Good luck.

FINDING A WARM PLACE TO LET BREAD DOUGH RISE

The ideal rising temperature for bread dough is between 80° and 90°F. If it is cooler, the rising is sluggish, if much hotter the yeast might burn itself out. If the thermostat in your home is set at 80°, you can put your bowl of dough anywhere. If your temperature is normal, a warm spot or high shelf in your kitchen might do, or you could turn on the heat in your oven at its lowest setting for 5 minutes, then turn it off and put the dough in. A friend of mine puts hers in the warming oven or on a heating pad at its lowest setting. My mother used to put her bowl of coffee-cake dough on a board on top of a radiator. I put mine on a sunny window ledge. In winter I put it on a shelf above an electric heating unit, or on top of my fridge.

While visiting at a summer cottage, I found that a perfect rising-place on a cool day was the seat of my car, which was parked in the sun. And one shivery morning in September I mixed my bread dough at dawn and went back to my warm, welcome bed. Like the slap of a frosty wet fish, the thought struck me that dough won't rise well in the cold. I got up, brought the covered bowl to my bed and tucked it under the electric blanket. Of course I slept again. Of course, the dough rose. And so did I, very quickly.

SOME HELPFUL THINGS TO KNOW ABOUT YEAST BAKING

Dough seems to rise better on a sunny day than on a dull one. If you want to speed up your yeast-baking time, you can use more yeast; 1 tablespoon of yeast to each cup of liquid, or 1 tablespoon to each 3 cups of flour. (Each packet contains 1 tablespoon.)

When my mother baked coffee cakes, she had to crumble a yeast cake and dissolve it in water. Now yeast is dry and comes in packets or in tins of various sizes. The yeast must be dissolved in lukewarm water (with a bit of sugar) before it is stirred into the other ingredients. Warm your mixing bowl with hot water before you pour in the lukewarm water to dissolve the yeast. Hannah and Eva and some of their Old Order Mennonite friends have discovered an easier and more economical way: they and I buy vacuum-packed Firmopan yeast, which is very fine and can simply be added with the flour. It should be kept in the freezer or eventually it will lose its rising power. The more yeast you keep in your house, the more likely you are to use it. I guarantee you'll enjoy using it, and so will all those with whom you share your bread.

Instead of plain water in the basic recipe, you can use milk, buttermilk, sour milk, fruit juices, or water in which potatoes have been boiled. Water gives a crisper crust; milk is more nutritious and makes a browner crust. (You can use powdered milk.) Potato water will give a coarser, slightly larger loaf. One or two eggs, lightly beaten, can be used as part of the liquid; they add flavour, colour, and delicacy.

As you stir in the flour, the ingredients cling, and the dough has elasticity; if it is kneaded, the bond becomes stronger; a soft, sticky dough can't be kneaded but will rise just the same when covered and put in a warm, draftless place.

You may find that a stated amount of flour or liquid in a recipe seems exactly right at one time, but not at another; this is because the absorptive quality of the flour varies with temperature and humidity. All you can do then is add a bit more flour or liquid until the dough is easy to handle. Better too moist than too dry. Don't be nervous, you'll soon get the feel of it and whack your dough around with abandon. Remember that bread-making is fun and therapeutic; be light-hearted about it and your bread will be light.

If you are interrupted while mixing or kneading your dough, don't worry about it; the dough will be easier to handle when you get back to it. Cover it if you're having a long-winded phone conversation. If the dough has risen smooth and puffy above the rim of your bowl and you can't carry on with the process for a while, don't let it run over and give you a sticky mess to clean up, simply punch the dough down and let it rise a second or even a third time. It will rise more quickly each time — but not forever. Nor will it rise much after you put it in the oven to be baked.

You can tell if your dough has risen enough by sticking your finger deeply into it (the fingertip test); if the dent stays, the dough is ready to be shaped into loaves or buns.

If you want a glaze on your bread or rolls, brush them before and just after baking with an egg yolk or white, or a whole egg, beaten with 1 or 2 tablespoons of water. But why bother?

If you want a hard crust, put a shallow pan of boiling water on the floor of the oven while baking your bread.

If your bread, richly brown in the oven and smelling like heaven, seems to be baked, take it out and tip it from the pan onto a rack; if then you discover that its bottom is pale, or if it does not give a hollow sound when you flick it with your finger, put it back in the pan and into the oven to bake a few minutes longer; no harm is done by the interruption. Yeast baking is much more accommodating than baking with baking powder or soda.

Do you say you don't have time to make bread? Do you have time to watch TV? Or play games? Or go shopping for what you don't need?

During the first years that I boarded with the Ingrahams in Neil's Harbour, there was no electricity, and no TV in the village. Clara May listened to a battery radio as she kneaded her bread or scrubbed floors. One day she lamented: "Can't play the radio no more, one o' grandchildern broke the switch; done it just for badment. Now we got no music and I can't listen to the stories. Ain't nobody in Neil's Harbour can fix it. It will have to be took down to Sydney." She shook her head. "Ye scarce git your own half raised up when grandchildern come round and beat up on things."

"That's how children is these days, don't seem to know how hard we work to git things noice," a visiting neighbour complained. "I always says there's no harder workin' women nowheres than in Neil's Harbour." She looked at me. "And I know because I been in Sydney to visit my daughter and I seen how easy they got it in town with electric and taps and milk comin' in bottles. Seems around here we's always cow huntin' and carryin' water."

Clara May went on, "We got lots more cooking too than in town, bakin' our own bread and preserving the berries we pick on the barrens. Then there's washing and scrubbing every day, sewing our clothes, knitting socks and mitts, making quilts, hooking mats. I ain't complaining, mind, I'm only telling you," she said quickly. "After having thirteen and two boarders I got it fair easy now with only eight home and Maggie soon leaving. Sometimes I's roight lonesome for them that's away. I'd rather be bakin' bread three times a week for all of they."

BASIC BREADS

NEIL'S HARBOUR WHITE BREAD

I've read dozens of recipes for making bread and I've tried quite a few but I don't like any as well as the one I got from Clara May in Neil's Harbour and have changed to suit my own hurried way. It is so good and so easy — try it some day when you're going to be home for 3 or 4 hours. You'll have 3 loaves or 6 "buns o' bread."

Into a large, warmed, pottery bowl (10 inches across and 6 inches deep) pour:

1 cup lukewarm water

In the water, dissolve:

1 teaspoon sugar

Over the water, sprinkle:

2 tablespoons yeast

Let stand while you drink your breakfast coffee — 10 minutes; by that time the yeast will have risen to the surface of the water. Stir till it's blended, making sure all the yeast is dissolved.

Into the yeast mixture, stir:

2 cups lukewarm water
½ cup sugar or less
1 heaping tablespoon salt
½ cup salad oil or melted shortening

Beat, then stir in, 1 cup at a time:

about 9 cups all-purpose flour

Mix till it requires muscle (you might add another ½ cup of water to work in the last 2 cupfuls of flour); rest, then keep on mixing till the dough hangs together and is easy to handle but floppy and inclined to be moist.

Scrape the dough onto a well-floured surface, sprinkle it with flour, and knead it; that is, gather the dough together in your hands then push it firmly away with the heels of your palms. Keep turning the dough, sprinkling on more flour — you might use a whole cupful. Keep kneading for several minutes — longer if you find it good therapy — till the dough seems smooth and elastic, though it might still have a few sticky spots.

Plop the dough back into the bowl, rub over it the dough that has stuck to your hands, and a sprinkling of flour. Loosely cover the bowl with waxed paper, a dish towel, or a piece of dry-cleaner's plastic, then a nice heavy sweater. Put the bowl in a warm, draftless place and let the dough rise 1 to 2 hours. It should be double its original size, puffed up smoothly over the top of the bowl. Use the finger-tip test (see page 4).

Punch the dough down with your hands to get rid of air bubbles. Divide the dough into 3 or 6 parts; scoop out one part, dredge it with flour, and shape it into a loaf or into 2 round, big, fat buns — as they do in Neil's Harbour. (I prefer the buns o' bread because the loaf can be torn apart to make two small loaves; also, when sliced with the torn part up, a slice fits better into my toaster.) Put the loaf or 2 buns into a thickly greased loaf pan, and do the same with the other portions of dough.

Cover the pans and let the dough rise again in the warm place till it is smooth and round over the tops of the pans — about an hour and slightly more.

Bake at 400°F for about 30 minutes. The baking smell will be divine. When the loaves are brown, top and bottom, remove them at once from the pans to a rack and let them cool, away from a draft — and from all impatient onlookers who love bread, hot from the oven, with butter melting into it. Oh, boy!

Though this bread is so popular that it won't last long if you make it accessible, you can easily freeze it and keep it.

If you like, you may vary each loaf that you make, or use some of the dough to make buns.

From this Basic Neil's Harbour Bread recipe you can make many interesting and delicious variations.

RAISIN BREAD

Everyone loves raisin bread.

If you want three loaves of raisin bread you have simply to add a pound or so of **raisins** to the bread dough when you are mixing in the flour. If you want only one or two loaves, you can add the raisins after the dough has risen and you've divided it: knead in a cupful of raisins per loaf, then put your loaf into the greased pan to rise.

ORANGE RAISIN BREAD

An easy way to make something special.

Use lukewarm **orange juice** instead of water in the Neil's Harbour recipe (or half of it). Add 2 tablespoons grated **orange rind** and 2 cups **raisins**. Add ½ to 1 cup **nuts**, too, if you want it to be even better. Bake as for Raisin Bread.

FRUIT ROLL

This is a beauty.

Roll the dough for 1 loaf an inch thick and about 6" x 9". Spread melted **butter** over the dough, then spread chopped **candied fruits** or fresh fruits or jam over it. Roll it as you would a jelly roll, seal it carefully round the edges and put it into a well-buttered pan to rise until doubled. Bake at 400°F for about 30 minutes, till done.

CINNAMON ROLL

Lovely for afternoon tea — or any time.

Roll the dough for 1 loaf an inch thick and about 6" x 9". Spread melted **butter** over the dough, then sprinkle it generously with white or brown **sugar** and **cinnamon** — **raisins** and chopped **nuts**, too, if you like. Roll it as you would a jelly roll and put it into a well-buttered bread pan to rise. Bake at 400°F for about 30 minutes.

FRUIT LOAF

Delicious and fancy-looking.

To the basic dough add 1 or 2 cups **mixed candied fruit**, chopped fine, 1 or 2 cups **raisins**, and 1 cup chopped **nuts**. Or knead ⅓ of the amount into 3 small loaves. Glaze the top with a slightly runny blend of icing sugar and water.

SPICE BREAD

Try it toasted with apple butter, honey, or jam.

Add 1 teaspoon each of **cinnamon** and **cloves**, and ½ teaspoon **nutmeg** or **ginger** when you mix your flour. Or knead spices into individual loaves.

SAVOURY BREADS

Use less sugar in the basic recipe when making these.

HERB BREAD

Wrap this in foil and reheat, sliced, with plain or garlic butter.

Knead into each loaf of basic dough 1 tablespoon of one or two different herbs: **summer savoury**, **marjoram**, **thyme**, **sage**, **basil**, **oregano**, **rosemary**, **cardamom**, **celery seed**, **dill seed** or snipped fresh **dill**, **parsley**. Or you might like to try a combination of herbs or seeds in each of 6 buns of bread. Have fun. Be daring.

CHEESE BREAD

Need I exclaim? You know how good cheese bread is.

Mix 2 or 3 cups shredded sharp **Cheddar cheese**, or chunks, into the basic bread dough, or knead 1 cup cheese into each loaf.

ONION BREAD

So good with salads or meats. Or cheese. Or anything.

Into the basic Neil's Harbour dough mix 2 or 3 cups minced **onion**, or lightly sautéed sliced onion, or 1 or 2 packages onion soup mix, or knead ⅓ of the amounts into each of 3 small loaves. If you use the soup mix, omit the salt in the recipe.

TOMATO–CELERY BREAD

If you want to mystify people, try this. It's nice for snacks.

In the Neil's Harbour Bread recipe (or part of it), substitute warm **tomato juice** for the water and add 1 or 2 tablespoons **celery seed**. Sprinkle each loaf with celery seed before baking, making the seeds stick by brushing the top of the loaf with lightly beaten egg.

CHEESE ROLL

Quite special.

Roll the dough for 1 loaf an inch thick, about 6" x 9". Spread melted **butter** over the dough; then spread 1 cup grated **cheese** over it. You might like to sprinkle on it **celery seed** or any pet flavour you may have (parsley is nice, too, or crisp bacon bits). Roll it up like a jelly roll and fit it into a well-buttered loaf pan to rise. Bake at 400°F or 30 minutes. Serve warm if you want the real glory of it.

ONION ROLL

Do the same as you did with the Cheese Roll, using 1 cup sautéed sliced **onions** or a combination of onions and cheese, or onions sprinkled with celery salt or sage.

BUTTERMILK BREAD

My absolute favourite. Whenever I have buttermilk, or sour milk that is fairly far advanced, I use it to make this tantalizingly cheesy-tasting bread; when it is toasted I savour every buttery mouthful.

To achieve this delight I merely substitute lukewarm buttermilk for the 2 cups of water in the Neil's Harbour Bread recipe; if I don't have 2 cups of milk, I use what I have with water to make up the difference, first scalding the milk, then adding the sugar, salt, and shortening, and letting it cool to lukewarm.

Dark Breads

By substituting darker flours for the all-purpose flour in the Neil's Harbour basic white bread recipe, you can experiment blithely and might achieve miracles. But there are a few things you should know before you start down that floury path.

1. Dark breads take longer to rise than white breads; where all-white might take 1½ hours, the dark might take 2 hours or more; to tell when it has risen enough use the finger-tip test (see page 4).

2. Dark breads don't double in bulk; the finished loaves will be smaller, more compact; you might want to use smaller loaf pans.

3. Whole-wheat flour is the only one that can be substituted completely for white flour. All other flours should be combined with at least an equal quantity of all-purpose or whole-wheat flour, alternating them in the mixing.

4. You might substitute brown sugar for white in the basic recipe, and a half-cup of molasses as part of your liquid.

WHOLE-WHEAT BREAD

Supposed to be less caloric and more nutritious than white bread. In the Neil's Harbour recipe use **whole-wheat flour** instead of all-purpose. That's all.

GRAHAM FLOUR BREAD

Use half **graham** and half **all-purpose flour** in the Neil's Harbour basic white bread recipe. Into individual loaves you might like to knead 1 cup chopped **mixed candied fruits**, or **pitted, chopped dates** , and 1 cup **chopped nuts**.

SOY-GRAHAM OR WHOLE-WHEAT OR CRACKED WHEAT BREAD

Follow the Neil's Harbour recipe using 1½ cups **soy flour**, 3½ cups **graham** or **whole-wheat flour**, and about 4 cups **all-purpose flour**. Very healthy.

RYE BREAD

Use half **rye** and half **all-purpose flour** in basic white bread recipe, and use ½ **cup molasses** as part of the liquid.

Rolls and Buns

Made with the same basic bread dough, they take less time to rise and to bake and seem a little more special. One batch of dough makes two loaves and one pan of buns; sometimes I make the whole batch into rolls, varying their shapes and their flavours.

PAN ROLLS

Easiest to make; soft, fluffy, with only a top and bottom crust.

After the dough has risen sufficiently in the bowl, grease a square cake pan with lots of shortening, and in it, side by side, place 16 or 25 little balls of dough about the size of golf or Ping-Pong balls. To get them round, dredge a piece of dough with flour, pull it into a long sausage shape, then break or cut off bits into flour; push a floured piece of dough through the circle made with a thumb and index finger, smoothing roundly into a ball. When the pan is filled put it away under wraps again till the dough has risen to double its size, nice and puffy. Pop the pan into a 425°F oven for 10 to 15 minutes till the buns are that beautiful colour, top and bottom. Cool them on a rack as soon as they come from the oven; serve hot or reheated. If you're going to pass them to people away from the table you might let butter melt onto their tops and you won't need to butter their tender sides when you pull them apart.

HAMBURGER AND HOT-DOG BUNS

These will make hot dogs and hamburgers sing. And they freeze better than those crumby store buns.

Roll the risen dough about ½ inch thick; for the hamburger buns take a fairly large-rimmed drinking glass or tuna tin and with it cut the dough into rounds; for the hot-dog buns cut the rolled dough into strips, cut the strips into hot-dog lengths; taper at the ends. Place the buns, not quite touching, on greased cookie sheets. Cover and let rise. Bake in a 425°F oven from 10 to 15 minutes. Cool on a rack. When people eat these, they'll probably ask if you'll bake some for their next party because hamburgers and hot dogs never tasted so good.

CHELSEA BUNS

Bevvy calls these **sticky buns**. One day at brunch at my cottage, a man guest ate 15 of my Chelseas; I was flattered — but his wife was so embarrassed that she left the table.

For a 9-inch square cake pan of buns use ⅓ of the Neil's Harbour White Bread recipe. On your floured kitchen counter, roll out the once-risen dough to about ⅓-inch thickness, about 7 inches wide and as long as it stretches to make the right width and thickness. Melt ½ cup **butter** in the cake pan (I prefer a Pyrex one), then spread ⅔ of the butter over the dough. Sprinkle about 1 cup **brown sugar** over the dough and ½ cup over the melted **butter** in the pan. Sprinkle the dough with **cinnamon** and a cup of **raisins**. Bits of finely chopped **orange rind** and half a cup of **nuts** are nice, too. Now roll up the dough as for a long, wobbly, jelly roll; cut inch-wide slices and place them cut-side up in the pan. You might have more than enough. Let the buns rise till they're double their original size; bake them at 400°F for about 20 minutes — watch them, they're precious. When they're a luscious, sticky, shiny, butterscotch brown, take them out and carefully tip them on a rack by putting the rack over the pan then turning it upside down over waxed paper; scrape up all the good taffy and dot it over any bare spots on the buns. Eat the buns while they're lukewarm.

One afternoon my mother and three of her girlfriends ate twenty-three after a game of bridge. Now you'll be thinking for sure I'm a bun-counter; I guess I am, but only because it pleases me when people enjoy them that much.

Chelsea buns can also be made in individual muffin tins — if you don't mind washing dishes.

Or: After rolling the dough and spreading soft butter over it, cover it with any kind of jam, or currants, dates, candied peel, honey, peanut butter, ground baked ham, cheese, onions, herbs, chocolate bits, walnuts, chili sauce or fruit relish, catsup, bar-becue sauce — whatever you like; roll it up like a jelly roll, cut in inch-thick pieces and place them touching on a greased pan or in muffin tins. Let rise and bake at 400°F for about 15 minutes.

VARIATIONS FOR ROLLS

Rolls can be made from any of the dough that is used for bread, white or dark. You can experiment with various trimmings. One morning I made 10 different kinds of buns simply by using a teaspoon of butter and a teaspoon of jam, honey, coconut and sugar, bacon bits, relish, and so on, in the bottom of muffin tins with a blob of dough on top. You should have seen how quickly they disappeared when a family of relatives came — everyone wanted to taste one bun of each kind, then several of their favourites.

ANOTHER VARIATION

After the dough has risen in the bowl, divide it into as many parts as you have fancies to experiment with. Mix or knead into the dough, shape as you please, let rise again and bake at 400°F for about 15 minutes.

Cinnamon, cocoa mixed with sugar, nuts, raisins or currants, dates and walnuts, cheese, crumbled crisp bacon, chopped fruit, crushed pineapple, chopped peel, candied ginger, cranberries: what else have you?

VARIATIONS IN SHAPE

CLOVER LEAF — put 3 small balls of dough together in a greased muffin tin.

TWIN ROLLS — put 2 small balls of dough together in a greased muffin tin.

CRESCENT ROLLS — roll the dough about ¼ inch thick, cut in wedge-shaped pieces; roll each piece from the wide outside edge towards the point. Curve slightly to make the crescent. You can roll jam into it if you like.

POCKET-BOOK ROLLS — cut out rounds of dough, butter one side and fold the other side over.

That's all I can think of but don't let me limit you — you probably have dozens of ideas I've never thought of; I have a tendency to stick to a good thing — my dear old basic recipe.

EVA'S WHITE BREAD
4 loaves

Eva's bread looks better than any I've ever seen; golden, crusty, high — perfect; and inside it is moist, has a smooth, even texture, and tastes good enough to eat without any trimmings.

1 teaspoon sugar
½ cup lukewarm water
1½ tablespoons yeast
2 cups hot water
3 tablespoons sugar
1 tablespoon salt
3 tablespoons lard
2 cups cold water
11 cups all-purpose flour
   (Eva uses her own wheat
   and has it ground: pure)

Dissolve 1 teaspoon sugar in ½ cup lukewarm water, add yeast, and let stand 10 minutes. Dissolve the 3 tablespoons sugar, salt, and lard in the 2 cups hot water. Add the cold water; and when the mixture is lukewarm, stir in the dissolved yeast and 7 cups of flour. Let stand 15 minutes. Add 4 more cups flour and work to a nice soft dough, not sticky. Don't be afraid to knead it well. Let it stand in a warm place, covered, in the bowl for 1½ hours till double in bulk. Work down, let stand another hour then divide into 4 well-buttered loaf pans. Let stand one hour or till well risen then bake at 350°F for 30 minutes — or until brown and with a hollow sound when you tap it.

EASY NO-KNEAD WHITE BREAD
2 loaves

Need I say more? You can stir this up in five minutes, let it rise for an hour, spoon it into two loaf pans, let rise again, then bake it and behold: light, crusty golden loaves. The best I've ever made.

2 cups water
½ cup vegetable oil
¼ cup sugar
1 teaspoon salt
2 eggs, slightly beaten
4½ cups flour
2 tablespoons instant or Firmopan yeast

Heat the water and oil together until warm — about 120°F. Pour the liquid into a large bowl and add sugar, salt, eggs, then 2 cups of the flour and the yeast. (If you don't have instant yeast, dissolve yeast granules in 1 cup lukewarm water and stir into the mixture.) Beat until smooth, then add remaining 2½ cups flour and stir to make a fairly soft batter. Cover the bowl with plastic wrap and let batter rise in a warm place until doubled in size.

Stir the dough and beat it a bit. Spoon it into two well-buttered loaf pans sprinkled with cornmeal. Cover and let rise again until doubled. Bake at 375°F for 30 to 35 minutes, or until the loaves are golden and sound hollow when lightly tapped. Remove immediately from the pans to a cooling rack.

PATTI'S MAGIC NO-KNEAD NEVER-FAIL WHITE BREAD
3 loaves

This is a simple, easy, amazing bread that can be poured into pans without kneading and can be used as a base for several fancy loaves or buns. It's almost too easy. When my niece Patti was twelve, she made these delicious crusty loaves of bread. Some evening when there's a half hour between your favourite TV programs, stir up a batch. Let the dough rest till you're ready to go to bed; punch it down, put it in loaf pans and into your fridge or a cold place. In the morning, take it out and let it rise to double in bulk; it will take a while to come up to room temperature — but you don't have to watch it, you can get on with your other work or reading your novel.

2 tablespoons yeast
3½ cups lukewarm water
½ cup shortening
⅓ cup sugar
1 teaspoon salt
2 eggs, beaten
7 cups flour

In a small bowl, dissolve yeast in ½ cup of the lukewarm water. Let stand 10 minutes. If you have Firmopan powdered yeast, simply add it with the flour and add ½ cup more water to dough. In a large bowl, pour remaining lukewarm water. Add shortening, sugar, salt, and eggs; pour in yeast and mix well. Add the flour a cup at a time, beating well after each addition, until you have a soft dough. Cover the bowl, set it in a warm place, and let dough rise until doubled, about 1 hour. Punch dough down; shape into 3 loaves and place in well-buttered loaf pans. Cover and let rise until dough reaches top of pan. Bake at 400°F for 30 minutes, or until loaves are golden and sound hollow when tapped.

And that's just the beginning. Instead of making three loaves, you might prefer to make any of the following buns and 1 loaf or 2 loaves. Also, to ease your conscience you might put in one or two cups of whole-wheat flour in place of 2 cups of white flour.

Chelsea buns, sticky buns, mince meat buns, savoury buns, pull buns, raisin or fruit loaves or doughnuts — all can be made with this moist, magic batter.

COFFEE CAN BREAD
2 loaves

If you really want to dazzle your friends try giving them round slices of bread. It's easy.

4 cups flour
1 tablespoon instant or Firmopan yeast
½ cup water
½ cup milk
½ cup vegetable oil
¼ cup sugar
1 teaspoon salt
2 eggs

Measure 1½ cups flour into mixing bowl and stir in yeast. (If you don't have instant or Firmopan yeast, dissolve yeast granules in the lukewarm water before adding flour.) Put water into saucepan with milk, oil, sugar, and salt. Heat until lukewarm — but not hot — and add to flour mixture; beat until smooth. Stir in eggs and remainder of flour and again beat until smooth and elastic. Divide dough between 2 well-buttered 1-pound coffee tins; cover with plastic lids. Let rise in warm place for about 35 minutes. The dough should rise almost to the top of the cans; remove lids and bake at 375°F for about 35 minutes or until browned. Let stand in cans until bread shrinks slightly from the sides and is easily removed.

BUTTERMILK SCONE LOAF
2 loaves

Chewy, light, with great flavour — especially when toasted.

2 cups buttermilk
½ teaspoon baking soda
¼ cup sugar
2 teaspoons salt
¼ cup shortening
½ cup lukewarm water
1 teaspoon sugar
1 tablespoon yeast
6 cups flour

Scald the buttermilk, stir in the baking soda, sugar, salt, and shortening; cool to lukewarm. Dissolve the yeast in the lukewarm water with 1 teaspoon sugar; stir into the lukewarm buttermilk mixture. Add the flour a cup at a time, beating well after each addition, until you have a soft dough. Cover the mixing bowl, set it in a warm place, and let the dough rise until doubled — about 1 hour. Punch the dough down, shape into loaves, and place in buttered loaf pans. (Or shape the dough into 3 large round balls and put them on a buttered cookie sheet.) Cover and let rise again until doubled. Bake at 400°F for about 30 minutes, or until loaves are golden.

CHEESE AND ONION ROLL
1 loaf

Roll out half the Buttermilk Scone dough — about ½ inch thick — spread with melted **butter**, then sprinkle with 1 cup chopped sautéed-till-soft **onions** and 1 cup graded **Cheddar cheese**. Roll as for a jelly roll, and fit into a buttered loaf pan. Cover and let rise until doubled. Bake at 400°F for about 40 minutes.

BUTTERMILK SCONES

Roll out half the Buttermilk Scone dough — about ½ inch thick — spread with melted **butter**, cut into 2-inch triangles, and place on a buttered cookie sheet; cover and let rise till puffy, then bake at 400°F for about 20 minutes — until scones are golden on top. Serve warm.

BUTTERMILK IN A RECIPE

Whenever I get a new cookbook, I go through it and put a B beside those recipes that need sour milk or buttermilk, a Y for a yeast dough, and a tic for a recipe I want to try.

To make buttermilk: Simply add ½ cup buttermilk to 1 quart fresh milk — or powdered — and let it stand at room temperature till it thickens, then refrigerate it.

To make sour milk: Pasteurized milk doesn't turn sour — it simply spoils and must be disposed of. Put 1 tablespoon lemon juice or white vinegar in the bottom of a cup, fill the cup with milk, stir and let stand at least 10 minutes to clabber.

Powdered skim milk may be used instead of regular milk: ¼ cup powder to 1 cup water. For ease in mixing, stir the powder in with the sifted dry ingredients and use lukewarm water for the specified amount of liquid.

DILL AND COTTAGE CHEESE BREAD

Almost since the Stratford Shakespearian Festival began, Claire Moore and four or five of her friends have come every year to one of the matinées. On their way home to Toronto they have side-tracked to my cottage for dinner or tea and a swim in the lake. One time Claire brought me a loaf of bread she had made; she gave me her dilly recipe and I've been treating myself to it ever since.

> 1 tablespoon yeast
> ½ cup lukewarm water
> 1 cup creamed cottage cheese at room temperature
> 1 tablespoon oil
> 2 tablespoons sugar
> 1 teaspoon salt
> 2 or 3 tablespoons minced onion (optional)
> 2 teaspoons dill seed or finely snipped fresh dill
> 1 egg, lightly beaten
> 2½ cups flour

Dissolve the yeast in lukewarm water. Beat in cottage cheese, oil, and sugar; add salt, onion, dill, and egg, stirring as you add them. Stir in flour gradually until the dough is quite stiff. Cover the bowl and let rise for about 2 hours or more. Stir down and turn into a well-buttered 8-inch casserole. Let rise again until light. Bake at 350°F for about 40 minutes, until the crust is crisp and brown.

BARBIE'S CHEESE BREAD
2 loaves

When Barbie wants to give her family a real treat, this is it.

2 cups milk
1 tablespoon soft shortening
1 tablespoon salt
2 tablespoons sugar
2½ cups finely grated strong
Cheddar cheese
2 tablespoons yeast
1 teaspoon sugar
½ cup lukewarm water
6 cups flour, approximately
1 teaspoon dry mustard
½ teaspoon paprika
Melted butter
¼ cup cheese

Scald the milk, add the shortening, salt, 2 tablespoons sugar, 2½ cups cheese; stir and cool to lukewarm. Dissolve the yeast and 1 teaspoon sugar in the ½ cup lukewarm water, let stand 10 minutes, and stir. Add to the milk mixture. Stir in the flour, one cupful at a time, with the mustard and paprika. When the dough is smooth and elastic, knead it, return it to the bowl, cover with a towel or plastic, and let rise in a warm place till doubled in bulk. Shape into loaves, let rise in buttered loaf pans till doubled. Bake in a 375°F oven for almost 40 minutes, covering loosely with aluminum foil if loaves start to brown too much on top. Remove from the oven, brush the tops with melted butter and sprinkle with ¼ cup grated cheese. Return to the oven for a moment to melt the cheese. Cool on a rack, then watch the loaves disappear.

MRS. BRUBACHER'S CHEESE LOAF
2 loaves

I bought a loaf of this at the Kitchener market and Mrs. Brubacher gave me her recipe. It is light and cheesy and irresistible — especially if it is warm or toasted.

In a saucepan mix and boil for 1 minute:

> **1¾ cups water**
> **2 teaspoons salt**
> **½ cup cornmeal**

Remove from heat, add and stir in:

> **2 tablespoons butter**
> **½ cup molasses**

Into a large bowl, pour:

> **½ cup lukewarm water**

In the water, dissolve:

> **1 teaspoon sugar**

Over water, sprinkle:

> **1 tablespoon yeast**

Let stand 10 minutes until yeast dissolves, then stir till yeast is blended. To yeast mixture add cornmeal mixture (when it has cooled to lukewarm).

One cupful at a time, add:

> **5 cups flour**

Stir until dough is right for kneading, adding more flour if necessary. Knead on surface covered with corn meal. Put the dough back into the bowl and let rise till double its bulk.

Cut into ¼-inch pieces:

¾ pound Cheddar cheese

Take the risen dough from the bowl and knead the cheese into it a bit at a time till all the cheese has been added. Shape into 2 loaves, put into greased loaf pans and let rise again till the dough is nicely rounded over the top of the pans. Bake at 350°F for about 40 minutes — or until the loaves are crusty and brown, top and bottom.

BACON AND CHEESE BREAD
1 loaf

You can vary this bread by adding herbs as well, but it's very good without.

1½ cups milk
¼ cup butter or oil
3½ cups flour
1 tablespoon Firmopan yeast
½ teaspoon salt
1 egg
1 cup grated Cheddar cheese
6 slices cooked bacon,
    crumbled

Heat milk and butter until the butter melts. Cool to lukewarm. Combine 2 cups of the flour, yeast, and salt, and add to milk mixture. Mix very well. Add egg and ½ cup flour and beat again. Stir in remaining flour, cheese, and bacon. Cover and refrigerate overnight or several hours until doubled in bulk. Punch down then scrape into a buttered casserole or loaf pan and let rise in a warm place until doubled. Bake at 350°F for about 50 minutes or until bread tests done. Cool on a rack.

HERB AND ONION CHEESE BREAD
1 loaf

This has so much flavour you'll make it again and again.

    1 tablespoon yeast
    1 cup lukewarm water
    1 egg, lightly beaten
    3 tablespoons melted butter
      or oil
    2 tablespoons sugar
    1 teaspoon salt
    1 teaspoon oregano
    1 teaspoon basil
    3 cups flour
    ½ cup minced onion
    1 cup grated cheese

In a large mixing bowl, dissolve the yeast in lukewarm water. Let stand 10 minutes, then stir in the egg, butter, sugar, salt, ½ teaspoon of the oregano, and ½ teaspoon of the basil. Add the flour half a cup at a time until dough is stiff enough to knead. Turn out on a floured board and knead until smooth and elastic. Put the dough back in the bowl. Cover and let rise in a warm place until doubled in bulk, about 1 hour.

Punch the dough down, then place in a large round buttered baking dish. Cover and let rise until doubled in bulk, about 1 hour. Combine remaining oregano and basil with onion and cheese; sprinkle over dough. Bake in 375°F oven for 45 minutes. Slice and eat while warm.

ALTERNATE METHOD: And very good too — in fact, I think, even better. Simply add the herbs, cheese, and onion to the yeast mixture before adding flour. Much simpler. You can sprinkle some more cheese on top of loaves, as well.

CHRISTMAS BREAD
2 loaves

This is so pretty to make at Christmas when you want to give a little something to your neighbours or a friend.

¼ cup lukewarm water
1 tablespoon yeast
½ cup milk, scalded
2 tablespoons softened butter
  or margarine
¼ cup sugar
1 teaspoon salt
1 egg, lightly beaten
½ cup chopped red maraschino cherries
  (or varicoloured peel)
1 tablespoon grated lemon peel (optional)
3½ to 4 cups all-purpose flour

Pour lukewarm water in a large bowl; stir in yeast and let stand until dissolved, about 10 minutes. Cool milk to lukewarm and stir into yeast mixture. Add butter, sugar, salt, and egg; stir in cherries, lemon peel, and half the flour, and mix well. Gradually add remaining flour and mix until the dough can be handled easily. Knead on a lightly floured surface until smooth and elastic. Plop back into the bowl, cover with plastic or waxed paper and a towel. Let rise in a warm place for 1½ to 2 hours — until doubled in bulk. Punch down and shape into 2 round loaves. Place on lightly buttered baking sheet or put into buttered loaf pans. Cover and let rise again until doubled. Bake at 350°F for 30 to 35 minutes. Frost with thin glaze of icing sugar and water.

CHRISTMAS BRAID

One year I got fancy and braided half the Christmas Bread dough. It looked great, and was much admired, but didn't taste any better than the loaf I made with the other half. Try it and see. It's fun and easy to do. Makes a nice little gift.

Mix the dough for Christmas Bread and let it rise in the bowl. Divide it in about half and put one part into a loaf pan to rise — unless you want 2 braids. Divide the other half into 3 and roll each part into a long strip about 18 inches long. Now simply braid the 3 strips as you would braid someone's hair. Pinch the ends together and tuck under. Place on a buttered cookie sheet and let rise until doubled and puffy. Bake at 350°F for about 30 minutes. While warm, glaze with a runny mixture of icing sugar and water. Decorate it, if you like, with cherries and slivered nuts. It should be served warm — reheat it wrapped in foil.

BREADS MADE WITH VARIOUS FLOURS AND GRAINS

It pleases me mightily to think that I have sent hundreds, maybe thousands of people on the way to glory. I mean the glory of making, baking, and eating their own delicious, miraculous bread. Many, many men and women keep telling me with pride and enthusiasm that they started making their own bread from the Neil's Harbour recipe in Food That Really Schmecks *and have gone on to its thirty variations of breads, buns, and rolls (pages 6-15 in this book).*

I don't always make an all-white bread myself. Having experimented with various flours and grains that are supposed to be more nutritious, I frequently make heavier, more gutsy, more flavourful loaves with whole-wheat flour, wheat germ, rolled oats, bran, cracked wheat, chopped grains, rye flour, soy flour, et cetera, in various combinations.

Try some of the following recipes. And don't be afraid to vary them — you'll have fun experimenting. Remember that yeast is magic.

QUICK AND EASY WHOLE-WHEAT BREAD
2 loaves

No kneading. These are rather solid loaves and not very high, but they have a fine texture and the assurance of being nutritious. If you want higher, lighter loaves, use half whole-wheat and half all-purpose flour — or whatever combination you like.

> 2 tablespoons yeast
> 3 cups lukewarm water
> ¼ cup molasses
> 1 or 2 tablespoons brown sugar
> 6 cups whole-wheat flour
>   (or half all-purpose or 4 and 2)
> 1 cup dry milk powder
> ½ cup wheat germ
> 2 teaspoons salt

Sprinkle the yeast on the water and let stand for about 10 minutes. Then add the molasses and sugar. Blend remaining ingredients well, then pour in the yeast mixture. Mix well until smooth. Turn into 2 well-buttered loaf pans. Let rise in a warm place until you despair of it ever getting any higher — at least 1 ½ hours. Bake at 375°F for 30 to 45 minutes.

STONE-MILLED OR CRACKED-WHEAT BREAD
2 loaves

This crunchy, moist, chewy bread will make you a compulsive eater.

    3 cups boiling water
    2 cups cracked wheat
    ½ cup shortening
    ½ cup brown sugar
    1 tablespoon salt
    2 tablespoons yeast
    1 teaspoon white sugar
    ½ cup lukewarm water
    5 or 6 cups all-purpose flour

Pour the boiling water over the cracked wheat. Add the shortening, brown sugar, and salt. Let cool to lukewarm. Dissolve the yeast and 1 teaspoon sugar in the ½ cup lukewarm water, then stir into cracked wheat mixture. Stir in the flour one cup at a time till you can handle the dough — it should be quite moist. Turn out on a well-floured board and knead until smooth — it will be too soft to be as elastic as the Neil's Harbour White Bread (p. 6). Return to the bowl and let rise in a warm place till it has almost doubled in bulk. Punch down and shape into loaves; place in greased pans and let rise until the dough reaches the tops of the pans. Bake at 400°F for about 45 minutes. Cool on a rack.

JEAN SALTER'S WHOLE-WHEAT AND CRACKED GRAIN BREAD WITH BRAN
4 loaves

This is the flavourful, nutritious, chewy bread I make most often.

4⅔ cups boiling water
2 cups cracked wheat, or Red River Cereal,
    or 5- or 7- or 12-grain cereal
1 cup bran
1 tablespoon salt
¼ cup vegetable oil
(I put in ½ cup molasses, Jean doesn't)
1½ cups dried skim milk powder (optional)
¼ cup wheat germ
1 teaspoon sugar
1 cup lukewarm water
2 tablespoons yeast
9½ cups whole-wheat flour

Pour boiling water on the cracked grain and bran; leave until lukewarm. Add salt, oil, molasses, skim milk powder, wheat germ, and stir. Dissolve the sugar in the lukewarm water, sprinkle the yeast on top, and let it stand for 10 minutes till the yeast floats; stir and add it to the lukewarm grain mixture. Add the whole-wheat flour 1 cup at a time, beating it in thoroughly at first then mixing till it is smooth. The dough should be quite soft. Turn it out on a floured surface, sprinkle flour over it, and knead it. You'll probably have sticky hands because the dough should be quite moist. When it feels smooth and all together, plop it back into the bowl to rise, covered, in a warm place, for 1½ hours or until doubled. Shape into 4 loaves and place in well-buttered pans. Let rise again until doubled. Bake in a 400°F oven for about 40 minutes. Remove from the pans and cool on a rack. Try to resist eating it hot with butter melting into it — that's when I eat 3 or 4 slices. And do I not gain weight? I won't tell you.

VIM AND VIGOUR BREAD
4 loaves

This should keep you healthy and enthusiastic.

3½ cups milk, scalded
2 cups rolled oats or wheat flakes
1 cup wheat germ
1 cup bran
½ cup honey or molasses
½ cup oil or shortening
1 rounded tablespoon salt
1 cup sunflower seeds, shelled
2 tablespoons yeast
1 teaspoon sugar
½ cup lukewarm water
8 or 9 cups whole-wheat flour or
   half whole-wheat, half all-purpose

Pour the scalded milk over the rolled oats, wheat germ, bran, honey, oil, salt, and sunflower seeds; let cool to lukewarm. Dissolve the yeast and sugar in the lukewarm water and proceed as in Jean Salter's recipe (previous page).

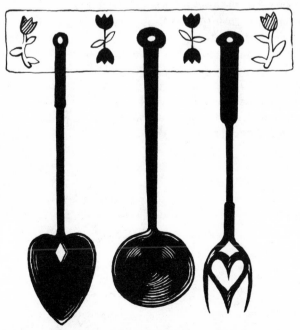

BARBIE'S NO-KNEADING BRAN BREAD
1 loaf

Great flavour. Barbie tosses this off in no time, and it's eaten almost as quickly. I mixed it in my food processor.

> **1 cup milk**
> **2 tablespoons butter**
> **3 tablespoons molasses**
> **1 teaspoon salt**
> **1½ cups bran**
> **1 tablespoon yeast**
> **1 teaspoon sugar**
> **½ cup lukewarm water**
> **2½ cups all-purpose flour**

Scald the milk, add the butter, molasses, salt, and bran; let cool to lukewarm. Dissolve the yeast with the sugar in the lukewarm water, let stand 10 minutes, stir, and add to the milk mixture. Stir in the flour, half a cup at a time. Beat it in until it is too stiff to beat then just mix it well. (I put everything in my food processor and let it whirl till a ball of dough was formed. Fantastic!) Cover the bowl, put it in a warm spot, covered, and let dough rise till it doubles, about 1½ hours. Stir it again and scrape the dough into a well-buttered loaf pan. Cover and let rise again until doubled. Bake in a 400°F oven for 30 minutes, or till it is brown on all sides. Remove at once from the pan, put on a rack to cool — then try to control its demise.

I like yeast things so much that I always want to double the recipe: the surplus can be a treat for my neighbour or tucked away in the freezer for that day when it will be a pleasant surprise to discover it.

HEALTHY AND FLAVOURFUL BREAD
2 loaves

Experiment when you make bread; this combination has good flavour and texture.

2 cups boiling water
2 cups rolled oats
½ cup wheat germ
1 cup bran
⅓ cup molasses
2 teaspoons salt
2 tablespoons sugar
⅓ cup oil
1 cup cold water
4 to 5 cups all-purpose flour
2 tablespoons instant or Firmopan yeast

Pour boiling water over rolled oats, wheat germ, and bran. Add the molasses, salt, sugar, oil, and cold water. When cooled to lukewarm, stir in the flour and yeast. (If you use regular yeast, you must let it rise for 10 minutes in ½ cup lukewarm water with 1 teaspoon sugar dissolved in it.) Keep stirring the dough until it is well blended. Knead it if you like but you don't have to. Cover the bowl and put it in a warm place until the dough rises to double. Divide it in two and shape into buns of bread or loaves and place in well-buttered loaf pans, or into three smaller pans. Let rise again until double then bake at 350°F for about 40 minutes or until golden and crisp with a hollow sound when you tap it. Slide the loaves onto a rack to cool and try to resist the temptation to eat while it is hot.

CORNMEAL BREAD
1 loaf

This has a gritty texture and a corny, bacon flavour that complements a green salad; it is especially wonderful when toasted.

Into a large bowl, pour:

½ cup lukewarm water

In the water, dissolve:

1 teaspoon sugar

Over water, sprinkle:

1 tablespoon yeast

Let stand 10 minutes until yeast dissolves, then stir till yeast is blended.

To yeast mixture, add:

2 tablespoons melted bacon fat (or butter)
½ cup lukewarm milk
2 tablespoons honey (or sugar)
2 teaspoons salt

Blend; then stir in:

2 cups or more all-purpose flour

Beat until smooth, then add:

½ cup cornmeal

Add enough additional flour to make a dough stiff enough to knead. Knead until smooth then let rise in the bowl in a warm place until doubled. Shape into a loaf and put it into a greased loaf pan. Cover and let rise again until doubled. Bake in a 375°F oven for about 30 minutes till it is crusty and brown.

CHEWY MOLASSES OATMEAL BREAD
2 loaves

This molasses-flavoured bread is so tasty that you will want to eat it with nothing but a spread of butter.

> **2 cups boiling water**
> **1 cup rolled oats**
> **1¼ teaspoons salt**
> **2 tablespoons shortening**
> **½ cup molasses**
> **4½ cups all-purpose flour — more or less**
> **1 tablespoon Firmopan yeast**

In a large mixing bowl, pour the boiling water over the oats, salt, and shortening; stir in the molasses and let the mixture cool to lukewarm. Stir in 1 or 2 cups flour with the yeast. Stir in the rest of the flour — enough to make a dough you can handle. On a floured surface, knead till it is smooth and elastic. Let rise, covered and in a warm place, until doubled in bulk. Punch down. Cut dough in half and shape each half into a loaf. Place in buttered loaf pans and let rise until above the rims of the pan. It might rise quickly but if it doesn't just let it sit until it comes up. Bake at 375°F for about 40 minutes — until the crust is crisp and the loaf has a hollow sound when you tap it. Don't underbake, but don't let it dry out, either.

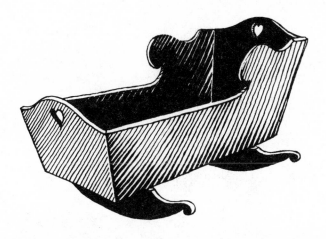

SCOTTISH ROLLED OATS BREAD
2 loaves

One time in Edinburgh I bought a loaf of oatmeal bread, hot from the oven. I had an English friend with me and we ate the whole loaf before it was cold. I've never been able to make a loaf that tasted as good — though this is a fair attempt.

> **2 cups boiling water**
> **2 cups rolled oats**
> **½ cup molasses**
> **1 tablespoon salt**
> **½ cup brown sugar**
> **½ cup shortening**
> **1 teaspoon sugar**
> **½ cup lukewarm water**
> **2 tablespoons yeast**
> **About 6 cups flour**
> **½ cup raisins (optional)**

Pour the boiling water over the rolled oats, stir, then add the molasses, salt, brown sugar, and shortening. Let stand till lukewarm. Dissolve sugar and yeast in lukewarm water. Let stand 10 minutes, then add to oats mixture. Stir in the flour — adding raisins if you like. Knead and proceed as for Chewy Molasses Oatmeal Bread.

LIBRARIAN'S BREAD

This is the recipe, exactly as it was given to me, with which I started baking bread. No wonder it was soggy and didn't rise very high. But I thought it had a wonderful flavour. Try it at your peril!

Mix:

> **4 cups whole-wheat flour**
> **4 cups white flour**
> **½ cup white or brown sugar**

1 tablespoon salt
1 cake yeast dissolved in ¼ cup water
1 quart lukewarm water or less
   (I'd say now at least 1½ cups less)

Cover with waxed paper and towel for 1½ to 2 hours. Stir it down, put it into greased pans, and let rise again. Bake at 350°F for 45 to 50 minutes.
   Try it and see what I mean.

MAGGIE'S MOLASSES PORRIDGE BREAD
3 loaves

This bread has that Down East molasses flavour, doesn't need kneading, is very moist, chewy, with a hard crust. Super. Maggie says, "You got to freeze this fast or they'll eat it before your back's turned." She often uses 3 or 4 cups of leftover porridge instead of water and oats.

2 cups boiling water
2 cups rolled oats
1 cup wheat germ
1 cup molasses
½ cup shortening
1½ tablespoons salt
1 teaspoon sugar
1 cup lukewarm water
2 tablespoons yeast
7½ cups all-purpose flour, or half whole-wheat
1½ cups lukewarm water or coffee

Pour the boiling water over the rolled oats, add the wheat germ, molasses, shortening, and salt; stir and let stand till the mixture is lukewarm. Dissolve the sugar in 1 cup lukewarm water, sprinkle the yeast over it, and let stand about 10 minutes, then stir it into the oats mixture. Stir in the flour, then add the 1½ cups lukewarm water and mix well. Let rise in a cold place overnight if you like, or let it rise in a warm place till it doubles in bulk. Spoon it into 3 buttered loaf pans and let rise to the top of the pans. Bake in a 400°F oven for about 45 minutes. Watch it. Take it out of the pans and cool on a rack.

COCOA RYE BREAD
2 or 3 loaves

Sophie says, "This moist dark rye bread has so much flavour you'll want to eat it just so."

  1 teaspoon sugar
  ½ cup lukewarm water
  2 tablespoons yeast
  1 cup molasses
  1 rounded tablespoon salt
  ¼ cup shortening or oil
  2½ cups lukewarm water
  4 cups rye flour
  ½ cup cocoa
  5 cups white or whole-wheat flour
  1 cup raisins (optional)
  1 cup walnuts (optional)

Dissolve the sugar in the ½ cup warm water and sprinkle the yeast over it; let stand for 10 minutes till the yeast rises, then stir. Add the molasses, salt, and shortening to the 2½ cups lukewarm water. Stir the rye flour and cocoa together then beat into the molasses mixture. Add the dissolved yeast and 1 cup of whole-wheat or white flour and beat until the dough is smooth. Keep adding flour until the dough is firm enough to turn out on a floured surface. Knead the rest of the flour into it till the dough is smooth and elastic. Put it back in the bowl, cover, and let rise in a warm place — it will double in about 2 hours. Punch it down, shape it into 2 or 3 loaves, and place in well-buttered loaf pans — or if you want round flatter loaves, put them into pie plates or on cookie sheets. Let rise again, about 1 hour. Bake in a 375°F oven for 35 to 40 minutes.

If you add the raisins and walnuts with the flour, you'll have a delicious tea bread.

BEER AND RYE BREAD
2 loaves

A firm, solid loaf with a subtle flavour.

1 tablespoon yeast
½ cup lukewarm water
1 teaspoon sugar
2 cups all-purpose flour
1 tablespoon salt
1 cup buttermilk
1 bottle beer
5 cups rye flour
3 tablespoons caraway seeds (optional)

Sprinkle the yeast over the water and sugar; let soften 10 minutes, then stir. Stir in ½ cup of the all-purpose flour and let stand until bubbles form. Add the salt, milk, beer, remaining flours, and caraway seeds, mixing the dough till it is thick. Knead on a lightly floured surface until smooth and elastic. Return to the bowl, cover, and let rise in a warm place until doubled, about 1½ hours. Punch down and form into 2 loaves. Place the loaves in buttered pans, cover, and let rise again until doubled. Bake in a 400°F oven for 15 minutes; reduce heat to 350°F and bake until the loaves test done, about 15 more minutes.

A VARIETY OF WONDERFUL YEASTABLES

In the winter when I can see snow on the roofs of the cottages at the other end of our frozen lake and there is snow on the ground and the spruce trees, when my lane is drifted in or too icy for visitors to drive through, that is when I get out my cookbooks and read until I can no longer resist making some of the recipes I've written there.

My favourite section of temptation is one with dozens of wonderful, interesting things to make with yeast dough. While the snow is falling outside and I am alone with my cats, I have lots of time to let dough rise and to enjoy the intoxicating aroma that makes my house smell like the best kind of bakery. That's when I make and eat — or freeze for future visitors — all sorts and shapes of buns, rolls, pretzels, pizzas, doughnuts, babas, kuchen, and English muffins.

Spring and fall are also good times to make yeast things, and there's nothing more pleasant on a day in summer when all the windows of your house are open and the neighbours on their patios say, "Gee, something smells good in your place."

Of course, baking is just the beginning. Eating is the best part.

MARY ANN MARTIN'S MAGIC BUNS, DOUGHNUTS, AND ROLLS

One hot summer day Eva and her sister Hannah took me to Mary Ann's farmhouse where the dough was rising; in a very short time we were gorging on perfect plump cream buns, Chelsea buns, long Johns, honey glazed doughnuts, and rolls.

1 teaspoon sugar
½ cup lukewarm water
2 tablespoons yeast
½ cup lard or shortening
3 cups water
¾ cup sugar
¾ teaspoon salt
2 eggs, beaten
6 or 7 cups all-purpose flour

Dissolve the teaspoon of sugar in the ½ cup lukewarm water, sprinkle the yeast over it, and let stand 10 minutes till the yeast rises, then stir. Blend the lard, 3 cups water, ¾ cup sugar, and salt; heat to lukewarm on the stove. Add the beaten eggs, then the dissolved yeast mixture. Add enough flour for a soft dough. Set in a warm place till doubled in bulk. Mary Ann put her dough in a plastic pail with a lid, and on that hot summer day it rose like magic. Punch the dough down and shape into whatever buns, rolls, or doughnuts you want to make. (See the recipes that follow.)

CREAM BUNS

Like those we used to get at the baker's shop after school. Super. Shape the pieces of dough into balls the size of a Ping-Pong ball, set on greased cookie sheets 2 inches apart, and let rise till doubled in size. Bake in a 400°F oven for about 15 minutes. Watch them, they shouldn't be tan. When they are cool, slit them almost in half and slather the bottom half with cream filling.

1 tablespoon shortening or butter
1 cup icing sugar
½ teaspoon vanilla
Pinch of salt
Warm water

Rub the shortening and sugar into crumbs, add the vanilla, salt, and enough warm water to make a soft spreading mixture. Mix with a knife then beat till light. Be generous when you slather it on the buns. They can be frozen.

CHELSEA BUNS

Mary Ann melted 3 tablespoons **butter** in a cake pan, generously sprinkled **brown sugar** and **raisins** over the bottom of the pan. She rolled out a piece of dough about ½ inch thick, slathered it with melted butter, sprinkled it with **brown sugar**, **cinnamon**, and **raisins**, then rolled it up like a jelly roll, cut it in pieces about 1 inch thick, dropped each piece cut side down into the pan till it was filled. She let it rise till at least doubled then baked it in a 350°F oven for about 25 minutes, till golden.

LONG JOHNS

Mary Ann rolled out some of her magic dough about ½ inch thick, cut it in strips 1" by 4", let the strips rise till doubled, then quickly fried them in hot, deep fat till they were golden brown. When they had cooled on a rack, she slit them lengthwise and not quite through, slathered them with the same **cream filling** she'd used for the cream buns, and sprinkled the tops with **icing sugar**.

Doughnuts with a Honey Glaze

Some of Mary Ann's dough was rolled and cut in circles with a doughnut cutter. The circles were left to rise till they were big and puffy, then fried in deep hot fat. When the doughnuts were cool she dipped them in the glaze:

1½ tablespoons honey
3½ tablespoons boiling water
1 cup icing sugar

Stir all the ingredients till blended. Dip the warm doughnuts into the warm glaze and let cool and dry on a rack.

Plain Buns

To make all this variety Mary Ann mixed up a second batch of dough. The dough she had left was rolled into small balls and dropped into greased muffin cups, allowed to rise, then was baked in a 400°F oven about 15 minutes, till golden. What a feasting day we had.

Mincemeat Buns

If you make — or buy — mincemeat for Christmas pies, save a cupful or two to make these buns: they are divine, tender, moist, and deliciously flavoured with pecans and Grand Marnier — or what have you. I use half of Mary Ann's Magic Buns recipe to the place where the dough has risen to double in the bowl. Then:

On a floured surface, roll a third of the dough into a rectangle about 12" by 9". Spread with 1 to 2 cups **mincemeat** and ½ cup chopped **pecans**, leaving a 1-inch border. Sprinkle the mincemeat with 1 or 2 tablespoons **orange liqueur** (Grand Marnier or Cointreau). Beginning at the long side, roll the rectangle like a jelly roll. Cut the roll into 1-inch slices with a very sharp knife and put each piece into a buttered muffin cup, cut side up. Let rise for an hour or so. Bake at 350°F for 20 to 25 minutes, until lightly browned.

GLAZE: Combine 1 cup **icing sugar** with 1½ tablespoons **warm water** and dribble some over each slightly cooled bun. They should be served warm.

EVA'S MINCEMEAT BUNS

Exactly the same as Mincemeat Buns but without the pecans and liqueur. And Eva makes her own mince. Instead of putting the slices into muffin cups, Eva puts them beside each other in a buttered cake pan and lets them rise. In the meantime she makes a syrup with ¾ cup **brown sugar**, 1 cup **water**, and **butter** the size of an egg — brought just to a boil, then cooled to lukewarm before pouring it over the risen slices in the pan. Baked in a 350°F oven for 20 to 25 minutes until golden, they are usually eaten before they are cool.

EVA'S STICKY BUNS, DOUGHNUTS, AND PULL BUNS

"I use Mary Ann's recipe for nearly everything I make except bread," Eva told me, "and sometimes when I'm in a hurry I even make it into bread."

EVA'S STICKY BUNS

These are divine; without exaggeration they are the best buns I have ever tasted.

Eva makes her sticky buns exactly as Mary Ann makes her Chelsea buns (p. 46), but instead of putting butter, sugar, and raisins in the bottom of the pan, Eva pours in enough **maple syrup** and **cream** to generously coat the pan about ¼ inch thick. She blends it a bit with her finger, puts the pan in the oven to warm it slightly, "Because I don't want to scare the dough by putting it in the cream and syrup cold from the fridge," Eva told me. Then let rise and bake as for Mary Ann's Chelsea buns.

EVA'S DOUGHNUTS

There's nothing like them; they are so good I could eat a million! One day in January, Eva told me she could hardly wait for the sap in the maple trees to start running. "But then you'll have to work so hard getting the syrup ready to sell," I said.

Eva smiled. "I don't mind the work. When the sap comes, it means spring is here."

And before it comes, Eva makes doughnuts and freezes them so she'll be ready to serve them with that first spring treat. One year she told me she made more than 700. "We like them so much dunked in fresh maple syrup and I won't have time to make them when I'm canning syrup."

Eva pats out Mary Ann's dough to ½ inch thickness, cuts it with a doughnut cutter with a hole in the middle, or in 2-inch squares, lets the doughnuts rise till they're puffy, then bakes them in deep fat till they're golden. (If you've never fried doughnuts, see frying method for Fastnachts on page 74.) She always serves them warm with maple syrup to dunk them in.

One day I took three city friends to Eva's house. We sat round her large oil-cloth-covered kitchen table and were very soon served a cup of tea. Eva put a nappie of maple syrup in front of each of us and passed round a dishful of warm golden doughnuts. My friends didn't know what to do with the syrup; there wasn't a spoon to accompany it. They looked around enquiringly until they saw me tear a doughnut in half and dunk it into the syrup.

They immediately followed my example and agreed on the way home that they had had the doughnut treat of a lifetime.

PULL BUNS (pictured on cover)

I think these are Eva and Hannah's favourite company thing. During the five years of the Great Cookie War between Procter & Gamble and Nabisco, when the lawyers, for whom the Mennonites had baked Rigglevake Cookies, came from Toronto, Ottawa, and New York, we'd sit round the kitchen table at Eva or Hannah's house and they would serve tea and bring on a great pan of Pull Buns for us to gorge on. We'd all keep plucking off buns until the great mound was diminished — and we weren't. (Read about the Cookie War in *Schmecks Appeal*.)

To make the buns — use Mary Ann's recipe. After the first rising in the bowl, roll a heaping tablespoon of dough in melted **butter**, then in a mixture of **sugar** and **cinnamon**. Put each piece of dough into a well-buttered angel food pan until the pan is a little over half full. Let it rise well over the top of the pan then bake in a 350°F oven for about 30 minutes or slightly more. Inverted on a large plate and served warm, these buns lured the patent lawyers from the cities many, many times.

NUTTY SWEET BUTTERY BUNS

Next time you make white bread or Mary Ann Martin's Magic Buns, try making some of the dough into these delicious tear-apart buns. Combine 1 cup **sugar**, ½ cup **finely chopped nuts**, and 2 teaspoons **cinnamon**; melt ½ cup **butter**. When the dough has risen in the bowl take out a good-sized gob of it and roll it into a cylinder about 1½ inches in diameter. Cut the roll into pieces the size of Ping Pong balls. Drop each ball into the melted butter to coat it, then into the sugar and walnut mixture. Place the coated balls in circles in a well buttered large pie or cake pan or heap them in a large loaf pan or tube pan. You may have several layers of balls. Sprinkle any remaining sugar mixture and butter on top. Cover and let rise until doubled. Bake at 375°F for about 20 minutes or slightly longer if you have several layers. Watch them so the sugar won't burn. Invert on a rack letting the pan rest over the buns for 2 minutes before removing it. Turn right side up on a serving plate and let the lucky eaters pull off the warm, sugary, luscious buns.

WHAT-HAVE-YOU BUNS

Experiment with whatever you have that appeals. Spread Mary Ann's dough with **jam** or **marmalade** or **ketchup** or **chutney**. Half the flour you use could be whole-wheat. Her magic recipe is full of surprises.

RUBY'S BUTTER PUFF ROLLS

The dough for these great-tasting rolls can be kept for a week in your fridge and baked whenever you want them, fresh from the oven. When you mix up Mary Ann Martin's magic dough, use ¼ cup less sugar and ¼ cup more shortening. Mix as in basic recipe.

Put the dough into your fridge or other cold place till you want to bake the rolls; it will rise slightly but should be covered. Break off pieces of cold dough, shape into balls, and put them into buttered muffin tins, or roll the balls of dough in melted butter and put them beside each other in a cake tin, or make any of Mary Ann's varieties. Let them rise for at least an hour, maybe longer. Bake at 400°F for about 15 minutes.

Grandma Stratton's Buns

When I came back from Arizona there was a tin box with my accumulated mail and in it I found half a dozen buns made by Lynn Wolff at least two weeks before; they were still moist and delicious. She enclosed her recipe which was the same as Mary Ann's, but had no eggs, 1 cup of lard, 4 cups of water, and 9 cups of flour. Lynn said, "In case you have aspirations, my father holds the record for eating the most fresh-out-of-the-oven buns, over a dozen in one sneaking session."

HONEY ROLLS

This makes a good-sized batch. If you like, you could make half the dough into Chelsea buns.

> **3 tablespoons lard**
> **1 cup boiling water**
> **1 tablespoon yeast**
> **¼ cup sugar**
> **1 teaspoon salt**
> **4 to 6 cups flour**
> **Soft butter**
> **Honey**

In a large bowl, melt the lard in the boiling water. Cool to lukewarm. Stir in yeast, sugar, and salt. Work in enough flour to make a soft, easily handled dough. Cover it and let it rise in a warm place until doubled in bulk, about 1 hour. Punch the dough down and roll out on a floured surface to ¼ inch thick rectangle. Spread the rectangle with a layer of soft butter and a heavy layer of honey. Roll it up like a jelly roll, then cut it into 1-inch thick slices. Place ¼ inch apart on a buttered baking sheet. Cover and let rise until doubled. Bake at 375°F for 20 to 25 minutes, or until brown. Remove from baking sheets immediately; cool on a rack.

RALPH'S HOT CROSS BUNS

My brother-in-law Ralph is always so pleased with his Hot Cross Buns that they are soon gone to his friends, relatives, and neighbours — and next day he whips up another batch.

> 1 cup milk
> ½ cup sugar
> 1½ teaspoons salt
> ¼ cup shortening
> 1 teaspoon sugar
> 1 tablespoon yeast
> ½ cup lukewarm water
> 2 eggs, beaten
> 2 cups all-purpose flour
> 1 tablespoon cinnamon
> ½ teaspoon cloves
> ¼ teaspoon nutmeg
> 3 cups whole-wheat flour
> 1 cup raisins or currants
> 1 cup mixed peel
>
> *Glaze*
> ½ cup water
> ¼ cup icing sugar

Scald the milk, add the ½ cup sugar, salt, and shortening; stir till they dissolve; cool to lukewarm. Sprinkle teaspoon sugar and the yeast over the lukewarm water and let rest for 10 minutes before stirring. Add the dissolved yeast to the milk mixture, stir in the beaten eggs, then beat in 2 cups of flour sifted with the spices; add the raisins and peel. Stir in the remaining flour then knead till the dough feels smooth and elastic. Plop the dough back into the bowl, cover it, and put it in a warm place to rise till double in size, about 1½ hours.

When risen, punch the dough down, place on a floured surface and roll it into a cylinder, not too skinny and about 18 inches long. Cut the roll into 18 pieces, roll each piece into a ball, and place about 2 inches apart on a buttered cookie sheet. Let rise to double again. With the back of a knife, indent lightly a cross on the top of each bun; let rise a few minutes more then bake at 400°F for about 10 minutes. As soon as you take them out of the oven, glaze the buns to give them a shine. Bring water and icing sugar to a boil, then simmer for 2 or 3 minutes. You don't have to make these only at Easter; they are wonderful any time.

EASTER BUNS

When my cat Cicely woke me at five o'clock on Good Friday morning, I decided to make Hot Cross Buns. But because I didn't have any peel to put in them, I used orange rind and called them Easter Buns. Good flavour, good texture; I ate six, took some to Belle and some to Norm and Ralph, having doubled the recipe.

1 cup milk
½ cup shortening or oil
¼ cup sugar
1 teaspoon salt
1 tablespoon yeast
¼ cup lukewarm water
1 egg, beaten
½ cup currants or raisins
Rind of 2 oranges, finely chopped
1 teaspoon nutmeg
3½ to 4 cups flour

Glaze:
3 tablespoons icing sugar
¼ cup water

Heat the milk to lukewarm. Pour into a large bowl, then stir in the shortening, sugar, salt, and then the yeast softened in warm water. Add the egg, currants, orange peel, and nutmeg, and enough flour to make a stiff dough. Knead until it feels smooth and springy. Plop it back in the mixing bowl, cover, set in a warm place, and let rise until doubled in bulk. Give it a couple more kneads, then roll the dough into two longish cylinders and cut off pieces to make 2-inch balls — or larger or smaller. Place dough balls on greased cookie sheets far enough apart so they won't collide. Cover and let them rise again until doubled. Bake at 400°F for about 15 minutes, or until golden. Watch them. While buns are baking, make the glaze. Stir together icing sugar and water and boil for one minute. Remove buns from oven and dip tops in glaze while hot. Cool on racks.

HILDA'S CHRISTMAS STOLLEN
4 stollen

For eighteen years — until her death — gentle Hilda Gremmel-
maier said she enjoyed cleaning my house every week. In No-
vember and early December, in her own kitchen, she made and
froze rich fruity stollen, until she had twenty — six for herself
and the rest to give to her friends and relations as a Christmas
treat. I was glad every year when she brought me one, tightly
wrapped in foil and Christmas paper. Hilda told me that in
Sachsen (now part of East Germany), where she was born, they
didn't make cookies at Christmas but saved all their money for
the goodies that went into the stollen.

1½ cups milk
1 tablespoon sugar
1 cup warm water
2 tablespoons yeast
8 cups all-purpose flour
1 pound unsalted butter
1 cup sugar
4 eggs
Grated peel of 1 lemon
Grated peel of 1 orange
1 teaspoon salt
1 teaspoon nutmeg
1 teaspoon coriander seeds, crushed
½ cup all-purpose flour
½ cup candied orange and citron peel
2 cups seedless raisins
1 cup almonds, chopped
¼ cup rum

Scald the milk and let cool to lukewarm. Dissolve the tablespoon
of sugar in the warm water, sprinkle the yeast over it, and let
stand 10 minutes, then stir well. Add the yeast mixture to the
lukewarm milk, then add 1 cup of flour. Beat well and let rise
in a warm place until light and bubbly. Cream the butter and
sugar, add the eggs one at a time, beating hard each time. Add
the grated lemon and orange peel and the salt. Add the creamed
mixture to the yeast mixture with the remaining 7 cups of flour,

nutmeg and coriander. Knead until smooth and elastic, about 15 minutes. Sprinkle the additional ½ cup flour over the candied orange and citron peel, raisins, and almonds. Mix well and knead into the dough with the rum until evenly distributed.

Let rise until double in bulk then punch down and divide the dough into 4 pieces. Roll each into a circle and spread with melted butter. Press down the centre of each circle with a wooden spoon handle, fold the circle over to double. Brush the top with melted butter, place on a greased baking sheet, cover and let rise until doubled. Bake at 350°F for 45 to 50 minutes. Cool on a rack then sprinkle with icing sugar. The rich slices are especially good when toasted.

DAMPFNODEL (Steamed Dumplings)

The last time I had supper with Bevvy and Dave, he said, "Did you ever have Dampfnodel yet? That is the best; that is really, really good."

Bevvy told me it is a dessert she makes on the day she bakes bread; she uses some of the bread dough. As soon as it has risen in the bowl to double its size, she works tablespoonfuls of the dough into smooth, round balls and lets them rise on a board until they are puffy.

Meanwhile she combines the ingredients for a syrup:

3 cups water
2 cups brown sugar
Butter the size of an egg
1 cup raisins — sometimes, not always

When the dumplings have risen to double their size she boils the syrup for 5 minutes, adds the raisins, then carefully drops in the dumplings, one at a time, covering and cooking slowly for 25 to 30 minutes without lifting the lid.

After trying them myself I can see what Dave means.

BABA AU RHUM

This favourite dessert of France is always greeted with exclamations, "You made babas! I thought they had to be imported." I tasted my first baba at a little café in the shadow of Sacré Coeur in Paris, and it wasn't as good as this recipe, which is not at all tricky, and the babas freeze perfectly.

> **1 tablespoon yeast**
> **¼ cup lukewarm water**
> **¼ cup milk**
> **½ cup butter**
> **½ teaspoon salt**
> **¼ cup sugar**
> **1 cup flour, sifted**
> **3 eggs at room temperature**
> **1 tablespoon rum**
> **½ cup chopped citron, mixed peel or currants**
> **Another ½ cup flour**

Dissolve the yeast in water. Heat the milk and butter, pour into a large bowl, stir in the salt and sugar; let cool to lukewarm then add the yeast. Stir in 1 cup flour and beat in the eggs, one at a time. Stir in the rum and fruit, then the ½ cup flour. Cover and let rise in a warm place until doubled. Spoon the bubbly batter into greased muffin tins or custard cups and let rise again until double. Bake in a 400°F oven for 10 minutes. Remove them from the pans and pour over them the following Rum Sauce. Or cool them, wrap them in foil, and freeze them, then heat and soak in the sauce.

> *Rum Sauce:*
> **1 cup brown sugar**
> **1 cup corn syrup**
> **½ cup water**
> **1 tablespoon butter**
> **½ cup rum**

Heat all but the rum to boiling point, stirring occasionally. Add the rum. Pour over the warm babas and let them soak up enough sauce to make them moist and spongy. They should be served warm. For a party I put mine in a wide dish that holds all of them and alongside have a glass bowl filled with whipped cream to blob over each serving. There's never a baba left.

BUTTERCAKES

Among the events of our very young lives was being taken to Toronto for the day in the Brisco, my father's first car. The drive took four hours — one way. But all I remember of the day in the city was standing in front of Child's Restaurant, watching the girl inside the window baking buttercakes on a big black pan, then going inside with Mother and Daddy, sitting at a table and eating the buttercakes, hot from the griddle and dripping with butter. We always said we wished we could eat them every day of our lives.

1½ cups milk, scalded
1½ teaspoons salt
2 tablespoons shortening
2 tablespoons sugar
1 teaspoon sugar
2 tablespoons yeast
½ cup lukewarm water
4½ cups flour

To the scalded milk, add the salt, shortening, 2 tablespoons sugar; stir then cool to lukewarm. Sprinkle the teaspoon of sugar and the yeast over the lukewarm water and let rest for 10 minutes before stirring and adding to the tepid milk mixture. Stir in the flour and beat it until you're almost tired. Cover the bowl of dough and let it stand in a warm place to rise until doubled. Now comes the magic moment! Scoop up as much dough as a tablespoon will hold, drop it on a lightly greased hot griddle or electric fry pan and cook until the bottom is golden, then flip it over and brown the other side. Bliss, heavenly bliss will follow when you break them apart and let the butter melt into them.

Too bad I didn't learn to make them when I was young and skinny.

KUCHA (Basic Dough)

From this fine, sweet, almost cake-like yeast dough, rolled out fairly thin, can be made a variety of delicious desserts, coffee cakes, butter horns, turnovers, crescent rolls, schnecken, kipfel, or nut rolls. Bevvy says it's appreciated at weddings, or funerals, or whenever a lot of folks come together to eat.

> **1 tablespoon yeast (2 if you're in a hurry)**
> **2 cups milk, scalded**
> **½ cup butter or margarine**
> **¾ cup sugar**
> **2 teaspoons salt**
> **Grated rind of ½ lemon (optional)**
> **Yolks of 2 eggs, or 1 whole egg, beaten**
> **About 6 cups all-purpose flour**

Sprinkle the yeast over ½ cup of the scalded milk cooled to lukewarm; let stand about 10 minutes then stir till dissolved. To the rest of the scalded milk add the butter, sugar, salt, and lemon rind. When cooled to lukewarm, add the egg yolks; stir in the yeast mixture and enough flour to make the dough easy to handle — it is better to put the dough into the fridge to stiffen than to put in too much flour. Knead the dough until smooth and elastic. Cover and let rise in a warm place until doubled in bulk — it will take at least 2 hours.

Now is the time to divide the dough for whatever you want to make of it: 1 dessert fruit kuchen and 2 dozen kipful, or a coffee cake and a batch of butter horns — whatever you fancy; the whole batch of dough would make enough fruit kuchen for 35 servings — or it would make 40 rolls. OR you could make one or two things and put the rest of the dough in a tightly covered bowl (that would allow some rising) into the fridge for 24 hours; then shape it as you please, let rise, and bake.

PLAIN KAFFEE KUCHA

After the Kucha dough has risen in the bowl spread some of it an inch thick in a shallow buttered pan or pie plate. Cover and let rise again. Melt enough **butter** to spread over the dough, sprinkle it with **sugar**, **cinnamon**, **chopped nuts** or **coconut**;

or crumbs made of ¼ cup **butter**, ½ cup **brown sugar**, and ¼ cup **flour**, with a sprinkling of **cinnamon** and dabs of **cream**. Bake in a 400°F oven for about 15 minutes.

FRUIT KUCHA

These refreshing, not-too-rich dessert squares of fruit-covered Kucha have as many variations as there are varieties of fruit.

After the Kucha dough has risen in the bowl, roll some of it as thin as you can and fit it into a well-greased flat pan or cookie sheet, 12" x 12", or thereabouts — the size doesn't matter. In parallel rows on top of the dough lay segments or halves of **apples**, **peaches**, **plums**, cooked **prunes**, **apricots**; or spread fairly generously over the dough pitted **cherries**, **blueberries**, **strawberries**, **raspberries**, **seedless grapes** — or whatever. Beat an **egg** lightly, add 1 tablespoon of **cream** or rich milk, and enough white **sugar** to make a thick, runny mixture that you can dribble over and around the fruit without having it run over the edges of the dough. Bake the Kucha at 425°F for 25 to 30 minutes; watch it till the crust is slightly brown on the bottom and the fruit is softish.

Now: remember the **egg whites** you had left from the Kucha dough? Beat them stiff, add 4 or 5 tablespoons **sugar** and spread the meringue over the fruit. Return to the oven long enough to slightly gild the meringue. Cut into squares, 4" x 4", if you want to serve them on a plate with a fork; or cut them smaller if they are firm enough to be held in your hand. Either way they'll be lovely good eating.

SCHNECKA (SNAILS)

When Kucha dough has risen, roll some of it to ¼ inch thickness in an oblong 9" x 18", or thereabouts. Spread with softened **butter**, sprinkle with **sugar**, **cinnamon**, and **raisins** or firm, fresh **berries**. Roll like a jelly roll, cut into inch-thick pieces and brush sides with melted **butter**. Place side by side in a well-buttered pan; brush tops with **butter**, sprinkle with **sugar** and **cinnamon**, and let rise until light. Bake at 375°F for about 25 minutes. Watch them. Cool on a rack.

Or, if you want more bother and even more commendable results, try baking the Schnecka in muffin tins with a teaspoon each of **butter**, **honey** or **corn syrup**, and a tablespoon of **brown sugar** with several neatly arranged **nuts** in the bottom of each section of the muffin tins. Let the Schnecka rise till more than double in bulk, then bake in a 375°F oven for about 25 minutes till nicely browned. Let cool for a moment, then remove Schnecka carefully.

TURNOVERS

After Kucha dough has risen, roll some of it ¼ inch thick, cut it into 4-inch squares and put a tablespoon of **jam** or **pie filling** in the centre of each square. Fold one corner over to the opposite corner and pinch the edges tightly together. Place on a greased sheet, let rise again, then bake in a 400°F oven until nicely browned.

KIPFEL

After Kucha dough has risen, roll some of it ¼ inch thick, cut into 3-inch squares, and put a tablespoon of **jam** or **pie filling** in the centre of each square. Pinch together the 4 corners of the square over the filling, wetting the edges and pinching them tightly to keep juices from running out. Place on a greased baking sheet, let rise again and bake in a 400°F oven until faintly browned.

CRESCENT ROLLS

After Kucha dough has risen, roll some of it into 9-inch rounds ¼ inch thick. Spread with softened **butter**, then cut the round into 4 wedge-shaped sections. Roll each section from the wide end to the opposite point. Curve to crescent shape, put on a greased pan, let rise again till puffy — about 2 hours. Bake at 400°F for about 15 minutes.

BUTTER HORNS

After the Kucha dough has risen, roll some of it into 9-inch rounds ¼ inch thick (or roll all of it if you want about 40 butter horns). Spread with softened **butter**, then with a jam or nut filling (made by creaming ¼ cup **butter** with ⅔ cup **sugar** and

⅔ cup finely ground, blanched **almonds** or ground **hazelnuts**; add just enough lightly beaten **egg** to make a spreadable paste). Cut the 9-inch Kucha round in 4 wedges. Roll each section from the wide end to the opposite point. Curve to crescent shape. Put on a greased tin, let rise again till puffy — about 2 hours. Bake at 375°F about 20 minutes. You can ice these with a plain butter icing if you want them fancy.

LARDY CAKES

When I visited Kath in Devon we would drive the six miles to Totnes to go shopping along its lovely ancient street. I could never resist the bake shops where I always bought richly delicious Lardy Cakes.

Take a piece of **proved dough** (that is, bread or bun dough that has risen). In Totnes it was always white. Roll it flat into a square. Dab pats of **lard** all over the dough. Scatter over this some **brown sugar**, **raisins**, and **currants**. You can also sprinkle on **grated nutmeg** and **cinnamon**, **chopped peel**, whatever you like and in any combination you like.

Then fold the corners into the centre like an envelope; then fold it in half.

Roll flat again and repeat the folding process twice more. Put into a greased tin and bake in a hot oven. This can also be cut into small squares or oblongs and baked on a baking sheet in a 400°F oven.

FLEISCH PIROSCHKY (Meat Buns)

Katie Enns told me the Russian Mennonites usually serve these
with borscht; I think they'd be good with a salad meal, too.

> 2 teaspoons salt
> ½ cup shortening
> 1 cup milk, scalded
> 1 teaspoon sugar
> ½ cup lukewarm water
> 1 tablespoon yeast
> 3 cups flour

Blend the salt and shortening with the scalded milk and let it
cool to lukewarm. Dissolve the sugar in the warm water, sprinkle the yeast over it and let it stand for about 10 minutes till the
yeast bubbles up; stir the yeast down, add it to the lukewarm
milk mixture, then stir in the flour to make a soft dough. Let it
rise, covered, in a draft-free, warm place, until doubled.

MEAT FILLING FOR PIROSCHKY

> 1 onion, chopped fine
> ½ tablespoon oil
> ½ tablespoon butter
> 2 cups cooked ground beef
> 1 or 2 hard-boiled eggs, chopped (optional)
> Salt and pepper
> Gravy or sour cream

Sauté the onion in the oil and butter until yellow; add to the
ground meat, eggs, salt, pepper, and enough gravy or sour
cream to moisten (or instead, use 1 cup mashed potatoes).

Pinch off pieces of dough and flatten them into rounds with
your hands. Put 1 tablespoon of filling on the round, seal the
edges together to form an oblong bun and place on a well-
greased cookie sheet. Let stand about 10 minutes then bake at
350°F for 25 to 30 minutes until golden brown.

APFEL PIROSCHKY FILLING

1½ cups shredded or sliced apples
1 tablespoon flour
⅓ cup sugar
½ teaspoon cinnamon
1 egg
¼ cup cream

Combine and beat well; proceed as for Meat Piroschky.

Cooked dried apples or cooked prunes and raisins could be used instead of the raw apples.

DOUBLE-DECKER BISCUITS

You can whip these up in a hurry if you want a treat for lunch.

1 tablespoon yeast
1 cup lukewarm milk
2 cups flour
1 tablespoon baking powder
2 tablespoons sugar
½ teaspoon salt
2 tablespoons melted butter or shortening

In a large mixing bowl, dissolve the yeast in the warm milk. Add the flour sifted with the baking powder, sugar, and salt. Then knead until well mixed. Roll out ¼ inch thick; cut in desired shape, dip in melted butter, and put one piece on top of another. Set on a well-buttered baking sheet. Cover and let rise in a warm place for about 1 hour. Bake at 400°F for 20 minutes, or until brown. Eat hot.

PIZZA

You can make pizza out of this dough. Let dough rise for 1 hour before you roll it out. Roll dough out to ¼ inch thick and flatten it into 2 pizza pans. Spread dough with **tomato sauce**, **meat**, **cheese** — or whatever you like on a pizza. Bake at 425°F for 12 minutes, or until crust is brown.

PIZZA

I live miles from a pizzeria; when I want pizza I make my own. It is fun, easy, and has many variations. Making the dough is a cinch — just like bread dough with whole-wheat flour. For 2 large pizzas:

>1 teaspoon sugar
>1½ cups lukewarm water
>1 tablespoon yeast
>3 tablespoons vegetable oil
>1 teaspoon salt
>4 cups flour, all-purpose or whole-wheat
>   or half of each

In a mixing bowl stir the sugar into the lukewarm water, sprinkle the yeast on top, let it stand for 10 minutes then stir thoroughly. Add the oil, salt, and flour till you have a stiff dough. You might need more flour. Turn it out on a floured surface and knead till it's elastic and quite firm. Plop it back into the bowl, cover it with plastic wrap or a dish towel, put it in a warm place free from drafts, and let it rise for a couple of hours, till it has more than doubled.

Meantime make the tomato sauce (unless you have some on hand):

>1 cup sliced onions
>2 tablespoons vegetable oil
>1 teaspoon salt
>1 teaspoon sugar
>1 teaspoon oregano
>½ teaspoon basil
>¼ cup chopped parsley
>1 can tomatoes, or equivalent in raw
>   or frozen ones

Cook the onions in the oil for 5 minutes, add the rest of the ingredients, and simmer for about 30 minutes, stirring occasionally. It should be thick enough to spread on the pizza dough when it is ready.

Now comes the fun and the ingenuity and the gutsy taste of the pizza. Divide the dough in half, form each half into a ball and flatten it, roll it if you like, or keep stretching it with your hands as they do it on the TV ads, till you have at least a 14-inch circle. Put it on a large enough cookie sheet, if you don't have a regular pizza pan, as I don't. Crimp the edge so it will be high enough to keep the filling from bubbling out. Turn up your oven to 400°F and put the dough in for 10 minutes.

Now the toppings. What do you like? What do you have? Try different things.

GROUND BEEF

I slather the **tomato sauce** over the pizza dough, cover it more or less with **crumbled ground beef** — raw or cooked — or leftover ground beef or other meat. Next I dot it all over with cheese: **Mozzarella** if I have it because it melts so quickly; **Cheddar** works well, too. Next I might have sliced **mushrooms**, slightly fried in **butter**, or some sliced ripe or green **olives**. Put it in the oven for about 20 minutes, enjoy its aroma, take it out, and serve it at once with a tossed salad.

The dough might be thicker than what you get in a pizzeria — the way my just-out-from-Italy friend used to make it when I visited her. She'd go to an Italian bakery on Dundas Street in Toronto, bring home a chunk of dough, and go on from there. Her pizzas were never spicy or hot and they were wonderful.

TOPPING FOR VEGETARIANS

I slather the dough with **tomato sauce**, spread a cup or more of **cheese** over it all — I've even used cottage cheese — then ripe **olives**, **green peppers**, **mushrooms**, sometimes **asparagus**, and a generous sprinkling of **Parmesan**. If my guests hadn't been vegetarians, I'd have sprinkled some bacon bits over it all.

PEPPERONI OR SAUSAGE TOPPING

But who has pepperoni? Smoked **pork sausage** cut in slices and nicely laid on the **tomato sauce**, or little **pork sausages** previously cooked, or even sliced **summer sausage** or **salami** cut in Vs and dotted on in a pattern then sprinkled with **cheese**.

ANCHOVY OR SARDINE TOPPING

Tomato sauce on the dough, then if you have **anchovies** use them and be fancy. I had none so instead I boned a tin of Canadian **sardines**, laid them neatly in a sunburst pattern round the outer edge of the pizza, put **olives** between the fish tails in the centre, sprinkled all with grated **cheese**, then **Parmesan.**

These are merely suggestions — look in your fridge or your cupboard for inspiration. If you come up with something super write it down in your little black book so you'll be able to make it again.

When the pizza comes out of the oven, all bubbly and smelling divinely, cut it in slices with a sharp knife, or if the crust is too crispy, cut it with bacon sheers. My pizzas are not always a perfect circle — but who cares — they taste good.

They're great heated over the next day, too (or you might freeze one and use it later). I put mine in my electric frying pan with the lid on to heat instead of drying it out in the oven. It was a bit of a squeeze but it worked. And was wonderful.

PRETZELS

When we were kids there was a scary little old man with a stubbly face, ruffled grey hair, and a dirty white apron who had a bakery of sorts near the Kitchener market. Mother would never buy anything from his shop, but sometimes Daddy used to go there and bring home big fat wonderful chewy hot pretzels. They were shiny brown on the top, sprinkled with coarse salt, soft in the middle, and suspiciously dark on the bottom. Daddy said the black wouldn't hurt us, the pretzels were baked in a brick oven. We blissfully ate them before they were cold.

I have been trying unsuccessfully ever since those long-ago days to find pretzels like them. Only once, in a store in Columbus, Ohio, I saw big hot pretzels and bought one to eat on the spot. But it lacked the chewy quality and flavour of the old man's.

Recently I've been trying to make some. They're not like the old man's either, but they're not bad. When I took them from my oven I couldn't resist eating one after another until I was horrified to realize I'd eaten nine. I took five to Belle, next door; she sceptically tried one, then immediately ate the rest.

> **1 cup milk, scalded**
> **¼ cup butter**
> **1½ tablespoons sugar**
> **1 teaspoon salt**
> **1 tablespoon yeast**
> **¼ cup lukewarm water**
> **2 eggs (save yolk of one for topping)**
> **3¾ cups flour or more**
> **2 tablespoons sugar**

To the scalded milk add the butter, sugar, and salt; let cool to lukewarm. Sprinkle the yeast over the lukewarm water and let stand for 10 minutes; stir well before blending it into the other tepid mixture. Beat one whole egg and the white of another and stir into the yeast mixture before adding the flour, one cup at a time, beating well after each addition, until it gets thick. Knead the dough on a floured board for several minutes; put it back in the bowl, cover, and let it rise in a warm place until doubled. Punch down, roll out on a floured surface until dough is about ¾ inch thick.

Now the fiddling starts — but you soon get the knack of it. Pinch off pieces of dough, roll each piece into a rope ¾ inches thick and about 8 inches long, and form a pretzel. Let them rise till they look puffy.

Put several quarts of water and 2 tablespoons sugar in a large pan, bring to a slow boil, drop in the pretzels one at a time, adding however many you have room for without touching each other. Simmer the pretzels for 5 minutes from the time they rise to the surface of the water, turning them once during the cooking. Lift them out of the water with an egg turner and place gently on a rack to drain. Beat the reserved egg yolk and lightly brush over the top of each pretzel, then sprinkle each with coarse salt.

When enough pretzels have been cooked to fill a buttered cookie sheet, bake them in a 400°F oven for about 15 to 20 minutes, or until the tops are golden brown and you can't wait any longer to get at them. They must be eaten fresh and hot.

If you get tired of shaping the pretzels, you could make circles, pinching the ends together; when baked they are not unlike bagels.

LESS-BOTHER PRETZELS

When Ernie Ritz was mayor of Wilmot township he told me
about the fat, chewy pretzels made by his son's wife, Kathryn.
They must be eaten hot from the oven — and that is no problem.

> 2 tablespoons yeast
> 1½ cups warm water
> 1½ teaspoons salt
> 4½ cups flour
> ¼ cup baking soda dissolved in 1 cup water
> Coarse salt

Dissolve the yeast in lukewarm water, letting stand about 10
minutes; add it and the salt to the flour, mix well, and let rise
about 15 minutes. Roll the dough into strips about 8 inches long,
place them in the soda solution for 2 minutes. Shape the strips
like pretzels, place them on a greased pan, sprinkle with coarse
salt, and bake them at 325°F for 10 minutes. Keep watching so
they won't dry out. Eat them at once or they're no good.

ARABIC OR PITA BREAD

For several years at Conestoga College, Barbie taught newcom-
ers to Canada how to speak English; her grateful pupils often
brought her presents. One day a Lebanese brought two puffy
loaves of Arabic bread made by his wife. Barbie and her family
liked the bread so well that she asked the man — in eloquent
sign language — if his wife would show her how to make some.
He seemed very pleased, kept smiling, nodding his head, and
next day brought her a large sackful of loaves — at least
twenty. Barbie persisted till she got her idea across and arranged to go to his home to see the bread being made. It was
quite simple: Barbie now makes Arabic bread quite often. She
makes about 30 loaves and freezes the surplus. You could try ⅓
of the recipe till you get the hang of it.

> 1 tablespoon sugar
> 6 cups lukewarm water
> 3 tablespoons yeast
> 12 cups all-purpose flour
> 2 tablespoons salt

Dissolve the sugar in the lukewarm water, sprinkle the yeast over it, and let stand until the yeast is bubbly. Put the flour and salt into a large bowl or plastic dishpan. Stir down the dissolved yeast and pour it into the flour; blend thoroughly. If it is sticky, add a bit more flour; if is too dry add more water. The dough should be smooth and firm but not stiff. Knead it a bit in the bowl. Leave it, covered, in a warm place and let the dough rise until doubled, about 1 hour.

Now, turn on the top element only of your oven and put a rack on the bottom position. Punch down and break off gobs of dough about the size of tennis balls. With a rolling pin, roll each ball on a floured surface until very thin, about ½ inch thick. Carefully slide the circles of dough on the lower rack in the oven at about 450°F degrees. You might have room for 4 at a time. While you are rolling out more, bake the ones in the oven for about 10 minutes, until the tops are lightly brown and puffy. Flip them over and let them brown on the other side. Place the baked loaves on a cloth and cover them with another cloth. (Barbie uses a tablecloth, which she doubles over them.) When the loaves are still warm, Patti and Ken like to push them down gently; they deflate like a balloon and are flat, 2-layered, and soft. (Like Yorkshire pudding with a top, bottom, and nothing in t' middle.)

They are best eaten warm, split, spread with butter on the inside, and cheese, or a cooked hamburger, or tomato, or hard-boiled egg mixture, or any sandwichy sort of thing. One loaf becomes like the outer parts of a sandwich but more interesting, delicious and chewy.

SOURDOUGH STARTER

Sourdough is a fun thing to have — besides a tangy good thing to eat in bread, rolls, biscuits, pancakes, etc. If you're out of yeast and miles from a supply, you can always start some as the pioneers did. Simply put 1 cup milk in a bowl or a crock (nothing metal) and let it stand at room temperature for 24 hours. Stir in 1 cup flour, cover the bowl with cheesecloth, and put it outside on your porch or balcony for several hours to expose it to the wild yeast cells that are floating around in the breeze. You could do this for several days to be sure you have a catch. (But not in the winter.) Bring it back into your kitchen and leave it, uncovered, in a warm place for several days, depending on how long it takes to bubble and smell sour. (If it starts to dry out, stir in a bit of tepid water.) You'll know when it's ready to use: it smells sour and bubbles like yeast.

Sometimes you have to try several times before you get a catch of wild yeast. If you grow impatient, you can always start sourdough by combining a tablespoon of regular yeast with the milk and flour, letting the mixture stand in a warm place till it bubbles and becomes sour, in about 48 hours.

Put the starter in a covered container with plenty of room for expansion and store it in your fridge — for years, if you keep it going. Each time you use it, you must replenish it by adding equal quantities of milk and flour and letting it stand in a warm place for 24 hours.

Sourdough starter should be used at least once a week (giving you a great excuse to keep making those lovely, flavourful things). If you don't use it for 2 or 3 weeks, spoon out and discard about half of it and replenish. It should improve with age. If you're going away on a holiday for several weeks and you can't take it with you, put it in your freezer and when you come home — happy day — get it out and let it stand in a warm place for 24 hours to get the yeast action started again.

BASIC SOURDOUGH to make PANCAKES, WAFFLES and HOT ROLLS

You'll say you've never had pancakes like these — or hot rolls, either. You can make these if you go on a camping trip; make or take your sourdough with you.

½ cup starter
2 cups milk
2 cups flour
2 eggs
2 tablespoons sugar
1 teaspoon salt
1 teaspoon baking soda

Blend the starter, milk, and flour, and leave at room temperature overnight or for several hours. Then add eggs, sugar, salt, and baking soda and mix well — but don't beat it.

PANCAKES

Drop large spoonfuls of the batter on a greased griddle. Turn over when the top side is full of broken bubbles and is no longer glossy. Serve with syrup and purr your pleasure. (You may stir in fresh or frozen blueberries if you like.)

WAFFLES

Use the same batter as for pancakes but add 2 tablespoons of salad oil before you drop the mixture on the waffle iron.

OATMEAL or WHOLE-WHEAT PANCAKES AND WAFFLES

Simply substitute 1 cup oatmeal or whole wheat for 1 cup of flour.

SOURDOUGH HOT ROLLS

Any leftover pancake batter? Make these delicious rolls.

To at least 1½ cups leftover pancake batter, or the whole recipe, stir in enough flour to form a stiff dough. Turn out on a floured board and knead until it is smooth and shiny. Put it in a bowl and let it rise in a warm place for about an hour. Punch it down, knead again, and roll out to ¾ inch thickness. Cut with a glass or tuna tin, dip top and bottom in melted butter, and place in greased baking pan. Cover, let rise until nearly double, another hour. Bake in a 375°F oven for about 30 minutes. Serve warm and buttery. Wow!

SOURDOUGH ENGLISH MUFFINS

Instead of dipping the hot rolls (above) in butter and baking them in the oven, dip the tops and bottoms in cornmeal, let rise till doubled, and bake on a frying pan or griddle for 8 minutes, each side.

SOURDOUGH BISCUITS

Once you start making sourdough biscuits, you can't stop. You have to keep using the sourdough. But don't worry: you won't *want* to stop.

Sourdough starter:
1 tablespoon yeast
2 cups flour
2 tablespoons sugar
2 cups water

Combine starter ingredients in a glass or pottery bowl, beat well. Cover with cheesecloth and let stand for 2 days in a warm place.

Biscuits:
1½ cups flour
2 teaspoons baking powder
¼ teaspoon baking soda
½ teaspoon salt
¼ cup butter or margarine
1 cup sourdough starter
Melted butter

Into a large bowl, sift dry ingredients together, cut in butter, and add starter. Mix well. Turn dough out on a lightly floured board and knead until satiny. Roll dough until it is ½ inch thick. Cut with a floured 3-inch round cutter and place biscuits in a well-buttered 9-inch square pan. Brush biscuits with melted butter, set in a warm place, cover, and let rise for about 1 hour. Bake at 425°F for 20 minutes, or until golden brown.

This is not the kind of sourdough the pioneers used in the wilderness — but it does make good biscuits.

To replenish starter: stir together 2 cups flour and 2 cups water. Stir into starter each time you make biscuits.

ENGLISH MUFFINS

I was thrilled to find I could easily make my own English Muffins instead of having to buy those weary old store packages.
Hot, tender, and moist between a crisp brown top and bottom,
they are failproof and freeze like a breeze — if they last that
long.

> 1 cup milk
> 1 tablespoon sugar
> 1½ teaspoons salt
> ¼ cup vegetable oil
> ½ cup lukewarm water
> 1 teaspoon sugar
> 1 tablespoon yeast
> 1 egg (optional)
> 4 cups all-purpose flour, whole-wheat, or both
> About 4 tablespoons cornmeal

Scald the milk, stir in the tablespoon of sugar, salt, and vegetable oil. Pour into a large bowl and let stand till tepid. In the ½
cup of lukewarm water, sprinkle the teaspoon of sugar and the
yeast and let stand for 10 minutes. Stir the yeast, then pour it
into the lukewarm milk mixture. Beat in the egg and 2 cups of
flour till the batter is smooth. Cover the bowl and let it stay in
a warm place until doubled and bubbly, about 1½ hours. Stir
down the bubbles and add the other 2 cups of flour, more or less,
till the dough is no longer sticky. Knead it on a floured surface
till it feels elastic — not dry or stiff, but not sticky, either.

Let it rise again until doubled. If you can't wait that long —
as I never can — sprinkle your surface with cornmeal and roll
out the dough to ¾ inch thickness. Sprinkle it with cornmeal,
and cut it in 3-inch rounds. With the leftover bits squeezed
together and cut, you'll have about 18 muffins. Cover and let
them double in size.

Heat a griddle or electric frying pan to medium, brush lightly
with shortening, and place the muffins on the hot surface.
Cover the pan. They should brown on one side in about 8 minutes, but watch them. Turn over and brown on the other side.
They'll puff up as they cook, be white on the sides, crisply
brown top and bottom. Heavenly smell. Cool them on a rack
until you can handle and eat them. Tear them apart, never cut
them. With butter melting into them, they need no embellish-
ment. If you can restrain yourself from eating all at a sitting,
they'll keep in your fridge for a week, tied in a plastic bag, and
be fresh when reheated. Also they're wonderful split and
toasted — and they freeze. But mine have never lasted that
long.

FASTNACHTS

The Lutherans call these Fastnachts and are supposed to eat them on Shrove Tuesday; the Mennonites call them Raised Doughnuts and will eat them any time. They're wonderful, warm or cold, dunked in maple syrup, or sprinkled with sugar.

1 tablespoon yeast
½ cup warm water
1 teaspoon sugar
1 cup hot mashed potatoes
1 cup sugar
1 cup lukewarm water that the potatoes
   were boiled in
1 cup all-purpose flour

Sprinkle yeast over warm water and sugar; let stand 10 minutes. Mix potatoes, sugar, potato water, and flour; add yeast. Let rise in a warm place for several hours.

Then add:

1 cup sugar
1 cup lukewarm water or milk
¾ cup melted butter
3 eggs, beaten
1 teaspoon salt
About 5 cups sifted flour for stiff dough

Mix all together, cover, and let rise in a warm place for an hour or two — till the dough has doubled in size. Knead lightly, adding more flour to make a stiff dough. Now, according to all my instructions, you're supposed to let the dough rise again for another hour or two, but that means you'd be fussing with these things all day. Figure it out: this would be its third rising, with another to come; I think at this point I'd be reckless and divide the dough in thirds and start rolling it out. What matters if you do have a few larger holes in your fastnachts? Take your choice, rise or roll. I'd try rolling the dough to about ¾-inch thickness. Fastnachts have a traditional diamond shape; cut them into diamonds with a knife. Another essential is to cut a slit across the top of each fastnacht with a sharp knife. Let the fastnachts rise, covered, in a warm place, till they're springy to the touch; when they're quite fat and puffy, drop them with the raised side down into fat that is hot enough to brown a bread cube — 375°F. (If you don't want that many fried cakes you might try baking some as rolls at 400°F.) Carefully — and one at a time — slide the risen fastnachts into the hot fat — at least 3 inches deep. Put in only 3 or 4 at a time, depending on the size of your pot. As they become golden on the bottom, turn them over, frying about 3 minutes to brown both sides. Lift out, let drip, then drain both sides on absorbent paper. While still warm, dip all sides into a glaze made of a runny mixture of honey and icing sugar, or simply shake each one in a paper bag with sugar or icing sugar, which will no doubt drip down your front as you eat these delectable morsels.

PEANUT-BUTTER BUNS

Having a party? These buns will be a pleasant treat — especially if it is a children's party. But why do we always associate peanut butter with children? Adults love it, too.

1 cup milk
½ cup sugar
1 teaspoon salt
¼ cup butter or margarine
2 tablespoons yeast
½ cup lukewarm water
2 eggs, beaten
4 cups flour
½ cup crunchy peanut butter
1 tablespoon melted butter

Scald the milk. Pour into a large mixing bowl, stir in the sugar, salt, and butter, then cool to lukewarm. In a small bowl, sprinkle yeast over lukewarm water and let stand 10 minutes. Stir yeast into milk mixture; add eggs, then add 3 cups of the flour. Beat until smooth, then stir in the remaining flour to make a stiff batter. Cover and let rise in a warm, draft-free place until batter has doubled in bulk, about one hour.

In a small bowl, blend peanut butter and melted butter. Stir batter down; stir peanut butter into batter to make a swirl effect. Spoon batter into 20 buttered muffin cups. Bake at 350°F for 20 to 25 minutes, or until golden. Serve warm.

YEAST COFFEE CAKES

When we were very young, we knew no other coffee cakes but those made with yeast. Mother loved coffee cakes and baked them often, always four at a time: two to keep and two to give away. Over the years she must have given hundreds. The keepers didn't last long; in our family of five, one would be gone at a sitting. But when Mother was living alone in the white house with green shutters she had built for herself, a coffee cake would often last for a week — with Mother enjoying it to the last stale crumb. I can still see her sitting at the end of her long kitchen daintily dipping the final slices into a cup of coffee and saying, "I know dunking isn't proper, but when you live alone you can do whatever you like."

MOTHER'S COFFEE CAKE

People who've eaten them say my mother made the best coffee cakes they ever tasted; they are light, moist, and covered with a baked-on crusty brown-sugar topping that sometimes formed deep little wells of candy which we three sisters always jostled for and Mother usually managed to slice in half to satisfy at least two of us. Over the years Mother must have given away hundreds of coffee cakes to friends and relations.

In:

½ cup lukewarm water

Dissolve:

1 teaspoon white sugar

Over the mixture, sprinkle:

1 tablespoon yeast

Let stand 10 minutes.

In a double boiler scald:

1 cup milk

In a mixing bowl put:

> **½ cup shortening**
> **⅛ cup sugar**
> **1 teaspoon salt**
> **2 eggs, well beaten**

Pour scalding milk into mixture and stir until shortening and sugar are dissolved.

Cool to lukewarm, then add:

1 cup lukewarm water and the yeast mixture

Sift and add:

3 cups all-purpose flour

Beat mixture till smooth.

One at a time, keep adding:

3½ cups more flour, mixing well to make a soft dough

Because Mother didn't like getting her hands sticky with dough, she kept stirring and stirring instead of kneading the dough for a few minutes on a floured board. Mother put the dough in the mixing bowl on a board or a pile of newspapers on her radiator to keep warm and to rise till the dough had doubled; then she divided it in 4, put it into greased cake pans, square or round, and let the dough rise again till doubled.

Carefully then, before baking, she put on the topping: ¼ cup melted **butter**, 1 cup **brown sugar**, and 1 tablespoon **cornstarch**, blended together over very low heat, thinning it if necessary with a bit of cream. While the mixture was warm, she spread it gently over the puffy tops of the coffeecakes, sprinkled a little brown sugar over top, then spread over that some "crumbs" made of 2 tablespoons of soft **butter**, about ¾ cup **brown sugar**, and ½ cup **flour**. She sprinkled that with **cinnamon** then put the cakes in the oven at 375°F for about 30 minutes (till they were done), watching them towards the last. The aroma of the coffee cakes baking is devastating. When we were young, we could hardly wait to get at them as they cooled on a rack. And often we didn't wait.

APPLE STREUSEL COFFEE CAKE

The first time I made this, I stretched the dough into a 13" x 9" pan — as I was supposed to — and after an hour in a warm place the dough hadn't risen more than a smidgeon! I quickly whipped up another batch and put it in a 9" x 9" pan, where it rose only slightly. But when I put both pans in the oven covered with topping, they rose about an inch and a half. Just a nice height for a comfortable bite.

½ cup milk
⅓ cup shortening
⅓ cup sugar
½ teaspoon salt
1 tablespoon Firmopan yeast
1 egg
2 to 2¼ cups flour
3 cups sliced apples

Topping:
½ cup brown sugar
½ cup flour
1 teaspoon cinnamon
¼ cup margarine or butter
½ cup chopped nuts

Heat the milk and shortening until the shortening melts. Let cool to lukewarm, then add the sugar, salt, yeast, egg, and 1 cup flour. Beat for several minutes then stir in the remaining flour to make a stiff batter. Press the dough into a greased pan (large or small — whichever you prefer — a flat or fat result). Cover and let rise in a warm place for about an hour until light and doubled in size (if you're luckier than I am). Arrange the apples over the cake. Mix the topping ingredients. Sprinkle over apples and bake at 375°F for about 20 minutes, or until golden brown. Serve it warm cut in squares or slices.

If you like, you can dispense with the apples and just have a Streusel Yeast Coffee Cake. Very good, too. And less bother. But the apples give it a nice seasonal touch. You can also use peaches or rhubarb, plums, or berries.

ONE-AT-A-TIME COFFEE CAKE

It never occurred to Mother to freeze or refrigerate a coffee cake before or after baking it as can be done with this cake. The dough can be divided to make three cakes — one to bake as soon as it's risen, the rest to keep in the fridge for up to a week and baked as you like. They won't ever become stale — unless you like dunking.

> 1½ **cups scalded milk, or boiling water,**
>   **or potato water**
> ½ **cup sugar**
> ½ **teaspoon salt**
> ⅓ **cup butter**
> 1 **tablespoon yeast**
> 2 **eggs**
> 6 **cups all-purpose flour**
> **Topping of your choice (see below)**

Pour the hot milk over the sugar, salt, and butter. Let cool to lukewarm. Stir in yeast, eggs, and flour, blending thoroughly. The dough — or part of it — may now be put in the fridge for several days and used as you please.

When ready to use, let rise until doubled. Divide into 3 parts. Pat each section into a buttered cake pan and let rise again. Cover with the topping of your choice (see below). Bake at 375°F for 30 minutes. (If you reserve some of the dough in your fridge it must be allowed to rise before putting into pans, then allowed to rise again.) Remove the cake from the pan and let cool on a rack before you slice it. Some people butter their slices of coffee cake, but if your topping is rich enough it is not necessary. Does anyone care about what is necessary?

TOPPINGS FOR COFFEE CAKES

STREUSEL TOPPING

Combine ½ cup **brown sugar** and ½ cup **flour**, then rub in ¼ cup **butter** along with finely grated **lemon or orange rind**, or ½ cup finely **chopped nuts**, or a teaspoon **cinnamon**, or any other flavour you fancy.

ROLLED OATS AND NUT STREUSEL

Combine 1 cup **brown sugar** with ¼ cup **flour**, ¼ cup **butter**, 1 cup **rolled oats**, and 1 cup **chopped nuts**.

HONEY TOPPING

Blend together ¼ cup soft **butter**, ¾ cup **icing sugar**, and 3 tablespoons **honey**. Sprinkle with nuts if you like.

SUGAR-CINNAMON TOPPING

If you want to be lazy, simply brush the top of the risen dough in the pan with melted butter, then sprinkle with white or brown sugar blended with cinnamon. It won't be as rich or as tasty but still quite acceptable.

PLUM CUSTARD COFFEE CAKE

Pat the coffee cake dough (above) ¼ inch thick into a round or square cake pan. Let it rise, then cover the risen dough with rows or circles of halved and stoned plums. Drizzle over them a well blended mixture of

> **½ cup sugar**
> **1 teaspoon cinnamon**
> **1 beaten egg**
> **½ cup cream**

Bake at 400°F 20 to 30 minutes, or until the crust is well baked and the plums are soft.

BREAD-DOUGH COFFEE CAKE

Next time you bake bread, treat yourself to a coffee cake by stretching some of the risen dough to fit a greased cake pan; brush the top with melted butter, and cover it with your favourite topping mixture (see previous page). Let it rise again and bake at 375°F for about 25 minutes.

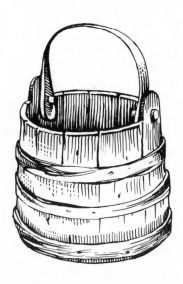

PRUNE AND APRICOT COFFEE CAKE

Your guests will probably say this is the best coffee cake they have ever tasted. Baked in a tube pan, it is moist, delicious, and impressive.

> ¾ cup dried apricots
> ¾ cup dried prunes
> 1 cup milk
> ¾ cup sugar
> ½ teaspoon salt
> 2 eggs
> ½ cup butter, softened
> 4½ cups flour, sifted
> 2 tablespoons yeast
> ½ cup lukewarm water
>
> *Topping:*
> ⅔ cup brown sugar
> 1 tablespoon flour
> 1 tablespoon cinnamon
> ¼ cup melted butter
> ⅓ cup chopped walnuts

Pour enough hot water over the apricots and prunes to cover them. Let stand for at least 5 minutes. Drain the fruits and chop finely. In a large mixing bowl, combine milk, sugar, salt, and eggs, and beat well. Add butter and 2 cups of the flour and beat until smooth. In a small bowl, sprinkle yeast over lukewarm water and stir until dissolved. Add yeast and 1 cup flour to milk mixture and beat for 3 minutes (easy with an electric mixer). Blend in remaining 1½ cups flour and chopped fruits. Pour ⅓ of the batter into a well-greased 10-inch tube pan. To make topping, combine brown sugar, flour, and cinnamon, and sprinkle ⅓ of it over the batter in the pan. Drizzle with ⅓ of the melted butter. Repeat layers 2 more times then sprinkle walnuts over top layer. Let rise for about 1 hour, or until double in bulk. Bake at 350°F for 45 minutes or until done. Cool in pan for about 30 minutes then remove to a rack.

INDEX